The Queen & I

Jeannette Charles

The Queen & I

PIATKUS

Dedication

**To my darling daughter, Carol,
who has been of great help
and encouragement to me.**

First published in 1986 by Judy Piatkus (Publishers) Ltd
5 Windmill Street, London W1P 1HS

British Library Cataloguing in Publication Data

Charles, Jeannette
The queen and I.
1. Charles, Jeannette 2. Entertainers——
Great Britain——Biography
I. Title
792.7 PN2598.C/

ISBN 0–86188–572–4

Phototypeset in 11/13pt Linotron Sabon by
Phoenix Photosetting, Chatham
Printed & bound in Great Britain by
Mackays of Chatham Ltd

CONTENTS

CHAPTER ONE

A Case of Mistaken Identity

The annual dilemma was looming – what on earth should I buy my husband for his birthday?

Ken travels a lot, so what about a toilet kit? No, I'd already bought him one of those. An umbrella? No, he had too many already. A tie pin? I'd bought him one, and he never used it. He wasn't a man who would wear jewellery, so what should I choose – ties, socks, a jumper? All the possibilities seemed boring and uninspired.

I was idly flicking through our local paper when I saw a discreet advertisement by an artist who was offering to paint portraits.

'Why not, for goodness' sake?' I thought. I'd been looking for something different, after all. So I rang up the artist, Jane Thornhill, and said I would very much like to have my portrait painted. I asked how much it would cost, and how many sittings would be needed.

'Can you give me an idea of what you look like and how old you are?' she asked.

I was a little taken aback at first – how many people think they look their age? – but there was one very easy way of describing my looks . . .

'Well, it's strange really,' I said, laughing. 'I'm in my early forties, and I've always been told I look like the Queen.'

We agreed a fee, and I went along to my first sitting in the studio at Jane's house. She started the portrait, and worked on it during my subsequent visits.

A local newspaper reporter used to pop into her studio regularly seeking news items, and he spotted the emerging portrait. He was curious enough about it to arrange to call in at the studio during one of my sittings. 'You look remarkably like the Queen,' he said. 'Have you ever been told that?'

I said I had, and so what? It was something that had been with me for as many years as I could remember, and didn't mean much. The reporter then asked Jane if he could use the story, but she asked him not to. I suppose she was trying to safeguard the confidentiality of a client.

I had about six sittings over the course of a few weeks. When the portrait was finished, Jane called me and said she was so delighted with it that she'd like to submit it to the Royal Academy Summer Exhibition together with two other paintings she'd done. 'It's one of my best pictures,' she said. I said I had no objection so long as she remembered it was my painting and returned it in time for me to give it to my husband for his birthday.

A few weeks later Jane telephoned me to say, 'They accepted your painting out of the three I entered and hung it for the exhibition, but now they say I've got to go and get it back.'

'Why?' I asked. 'Because they thought it was the Queen.'

'Well, what difference does that make?'

'A lot, apparently. The people at the Royal Academy contacted Buckingham Palace and were told it couldn't be a portrait of the Queen because she hadn't given a sitting. They think I've copied a photograph or painted it from memory. I've explained that's not the case, and that it was you who sat for the portrait, but they still say they can't hang it and I've got to go and get it back.'

The next day Jane was on the telephone again. 'I'm at the Royal Academy,' she said, 'surrounded by journalists who want to come and talk to you.'

'What on earth for?' I asked.

'Because they've seen the portrait and they say you look remarkably like the Queen. They think it's a great story and they want to interview you.'

I thought it was rather funny to receive a call from David Thurlow of the *Daily Express* who came to my house to interview me and take me on a walkabout in Chelmsford, the nearest town to my home, to be photographed in the streets there.

We used to take the *Express* in those days, and every morning my husband would bring it upstairs to me with a cup of tea for me to drink in bed. I'll never forget the expression on his face as he came into our room one day with the newspaper open in his hands.

'What the hell have you been doing?' he asked.

I was taken aback, forgetting the photo session for a moment. 'What are you talking about?' I said, surprised, then he laid the paper before me. There was a photograph of me under the headline 'No, she's NOT the Queen', and a story about my likeness to royalty. On the facing page there was the headline 'Yes, this *is* the Queen', and a story about Her Majesty being entertained by Queen Juliana of the Netherlands.

I had told Ken about the interview, but the coverage it received had clearly surprised and shocked him. It surprised me, too. I sat looking at the paper for a long time. Of course, I'd known the *Express* would probably use the story and the photographs but when I saw myself in print for the first time, and under banner headlines, I was stunned. I felt as if someone had knocked me over the head.

From that moment my life was to change irrevocably. The telephone rang and rang. Sometimes I feel as if it has never stopped ringing. People wanted to interview me for local papers, national papers, magazines and radio programmes around the world. For a while it felt totally unreal – I couldn't believe it was really happening to me. I was excited and tearful by turns.

My two sons were away at boarding school but my daughter, Carol, went to a local school, and I had to take her there in the mornings and collect her in the afternoons. It seemed every time I stepped out of my door, people were waiting to pounce on me, notepads and tape recorders at the ready. I'd glance out of the window and there'd be reporters hanging about in the street. If I left the house to go up the road, I'd camouflage myself in an old mac but still they'd spot me and ask me questions: about my youth, about being mistaken for the Queen. It was exciting but annoying at the same time.

Once I'd recovered from the initial shock, I thought it would be a nine-day wonder. I was wrong. Instead, my likeness to the Queen has resulted in what I call my second career, which so far has lasted for fourteen years. I've become a professional model and variety artist, and have travelled the world to be consistently fêted in royal fashion. It's like a wonderful dream that goes on and on.

CHAPTER TWO

Double Trouble

As a child I dreamt of becoming famous as a great actress in the theatre, and my ambitions towards the stage were fostered and encouraged. Every time my elder sister, Marie, and I went on holiday or to a resort town – Ramsgate, Brighton, Southend or wherever – our mother would enter us in talent shows. I had a sailor suit and would wear it to perform a sailor's hornpipe. I also had a gypsy outfit complete with tambourine, in which I would dress up. My sister's specialities were ballet dancing and singing, while I was good at tap dancing and, of all things, doing impressions. We loved putting our talents to use on stage, often winning money or prizes, but I had no idea that these early successes were just a foretaste of greater things to come.

I grew up in Wembley, north London, in the years before the Second World War, a time I look back on with many fond memories. Dad had a café-restaurant and, although we were not well-to-do, we were comfortable enough as there was always enough money for trips to the circus, theatre, and pantomime.

Marie was two years older than me, and our younger sister, Delinda, was born ten years after me. The three of us were very close, and we still are.

Dad had joined the Army at thirteen and became a chef with a considerable reputation. During the Second World War he was chef to the senior allied commanders, and was finally personal chef to Field Marshall Earl Alexander of Tunis when he was Allied Commander in Chief of Mediterranean forces. At the end of the war, Earl Alexander went off to serve as Governor-General of Canada, and wanted Dad to go with him as the household chef. But this would have meant my mother also working in the Governor-General's mansion, as a maid, and she didn't want to do that. For Mother had never worked outside the home. She had married when she was seventeen, she saw her role as looking after our home and the children, and that's exactly what she did. So Dad left the army to open up his café-restaurant. He seemed very happy doing that, and I don't think he ever regretted not going to Canada.

I never actually met Dad's parents, though they were Londoners. Mother was a member of the Kool family, the cigar and cigarette people. Her mother was originally Dutch Jewish, and her husband was Polish. In the summer of 1939, they had gone to Amsterdam on a holiday, visiting relatives. The war broke out while they were there, and they could not get back to England. Sadly, they died in a wartime bombing raid.

Every once in a while, someone in the family would comment on my resemblance to the young Princess Elizabeth, who was about a year and a half older than me. This similarity was enhanced when Mum would knit a sweater or a hat for me modelled on a style the Princess had been photographed wearing. Knitting patterns clearly based on the classic styles the Royal Family favoured were readily available in those days, yet royalty were always studied from a respectful distance, set on a pedestal in a way they do not seem to be any more. I can remember looking in mirrors as a teenager and seeing a royal likeness gazing back at me, and it was a bit of a giggle to have boys shouting, 'Princess Elizabeth!' as I walked home from school.

I went to Wembley High School. I loved it there, and always did well, even if our education in the wartime years was interrupted each time bombing raids forced us into the underground shelter. Those were frightening moments, but all in all my schooldays really were the happiest days of my life.

Not so pleasant was the occasion towards the end of the war when my mother and I took a boat trip along the Thames to Greenwich. We were walking up the great green slope of Greenwich Park towards the Observatory when we saw a photographer at the top of it, his tripod set up, taking pictures of a model. He noticed us and called out, 'I'm doing a spread for a magazine. Your little girl looks like Princess Elizabeth. Let's have her over here.'

My mother went scarlet with embarrassment, grabbed my hand, and ran like mad to get away. She was shocked, and I felt strangely guilty. (I think mother was horrified at the prospect of having a photograph of her daughter in a magazine because she looked like Princess Elizabeth.) We didn't stop running until we were well out of sight. I imagine the photographer kicked himself for missing the scoop of his life – a royal princess incognito in her ancestor's park.

When I left Wembley High School, I got a job as a typist at Odhams Press, hoping that one day I might become a journalist. The *People* newspaper was printed there in those days, and I can vividly recall how excited I used to be seeing that grand old newspaperman Hannan

Swaffer walking back and forth near my desk. He dressed in dark, eccentric clothes, had a great, magisterial presence, and was very courteous and kind to me. He often stopped to talk and one day he said, 'My dear girl, you have a great future ahead of you.' I don't know why he said it. I was very young and extremely shy, and I didn't know how to reply. He was right, but the wonderful future he prophesied was to take a long time to materialise.

Marie and I decided, shortly after the war, to go over and see if we could trace Mother's surviving relatives. We caught the ferry at Harwich and went below to our cabin to sleep the night away as we sailed to the Hook of Holland. When we docked at about six in the morning, I felt seasick and was looking forward to getting ashore. We gathered up our bags and headed for the gangplank. About halfway down something very strange happened – people on the quayside started shouting, cheering, clapping, and waving.

My immediate reaction was to look behind me to see who they had spotted. When I heard someone shout 'Princess Elizabeth!' the truth dawned: they were waving and shouting at me.

Once again, I felt terribly guilty and embarrassed. I blushed right to the roots of my hair. Marie could see how uncomfortable I felt but she thought it was very funny and was falling all over the place, laughing. It probably was funny to see me wilting with embarrassment, trying to make myself invisible, but I can still remember that awful creeping feeling of shame as if I had done something wrong, deliberately deceived the waiting crowd.

As I got to the bottom of the gangplank, the chorus of greetings reached a crescendo. A lady touched me on the arm and said, 'You are the Princess Elizabeth, no?' A young girl came up and curtsied to me. I wanted to die. I grabbed my bag and ran as fast as I could to the bus. Marie raced along behind me, still hooting with laughter. I found a seat right at the back of the bus and huddled into it.

Looking back on the moment, I can see the crowd's overwhelming reception which so terrified me at the time, was motivated by genuine affection. Our royal family and the Dutch royals have always been close, and never more so than during the war when George VI gave sanctuary to the royal refugees from Holland after the German invasion. The English royal family were held in high esteem as a result, hence the undeserved warmth of my reception. No wonder I felt guilty!

We found some of mother's family, an uncle and aunt who ran a hardware store in one of Amsterdam's main streets. I remember they tried to fix me up with a cousin. It was staged like an arranged royal betrothal. We were left in a room together but neither of us liked the other so it didn't come to anything. Our Dutch relatives agreed I could double for Princess Elizabeth, but there was no more public recognition. We stayed in small bed and breakfast guesthouses and I kept what I believe is now called a low profile.

But more double trouble awaited me when I took my younger sister, Delinda with me on a train tour of Italy. I was seventeen and Delinda was seven. Our first stop was in Florence, where we stayed at a *pensione* owned by the parents of a penfriend of mine. Word soon got around the young males of the neighbourhood that a girl who looked like Princess Elizabeth was staying there, and we had a succession of callers who just wanted to get a peek at the Princess's lookalike. It was quite ridiculous, and the persistent callers eventually became a real nuisance to my friend's parents.

Delinda and I went on to Naples where at the railway station, we were surrounded by a gang of teenage boys, all jabbering away. I did not understand Italian but I could pick out two words which kept recurring! *Principessa Elisabetta.* What else they were saying I don't know, but their interest in me was obvious. They gathered around very close and started to touch me, tugging at my clothes. I was becoming more frightened by the minute, and Delinda clung to me, appalled. Suddenly, from nowhere, a woman appeared, waving an umbrella above her head like a battleaxe. She put the gang to rout, insisting they leave us alone.

Our rescuer turned out to be an English lady teacher who spoke fluent Italian. She told us the boys had read that Princess Margaret had been in the area a short while before and had assumed that her sister had now turned up.

Our grand tour included the Isle of Capri, where we were taken in rowing boats through the fabulous Blue Grotto. It's the most beautiful place I have ever set eyes on, lit by arc lights so that you can see all the way to the bottom of the sea. The boatmen played the British national anthem on their mandolins, and I assumed this was because there were a lot of English people in the tour party until an American, who understood Italian, said the boatmen, who had escorted Princess Margaret around the Grotto only a few days before, were convinced I was Princess Elizabeth. When Delinda and I disembarked, the boatmen were all smiles and gave us a big round of applause.

We stayed in youth hostels and cheap *pensiones* all over the country, but the Italians were not going to be fooled by that. They obviously thought it was all part of our royal cover.

Perhaps my most enduring memory of this particular trip concerns Mario. A young waiter at a roadside café in Sorrento, he was pouring me some coffee when he happened to look into my face. His jaw dropped, and he stared at me, goggle-eyed. Unfortunately, he was still pouring the coffee. It filled my cup, then my saucer, then flowed all over the tablecloth and finally cascaded into my lap. The proprietor came out, screaming at Mario, really giving him a hard time. It turned out that the young waiter had also heard of Princess Margaret's being in the area with her entourage, and believed they had turned up in his café.

Mario, however, was a typical Italian male, ready to take his chance and fall in love with any girl he met, even if she wasn't a princess. He recovered his poise enough to obtain my address, and later wrote to me. His first two letters I saw. They were full of declarations of love, and he asked me outright to marry him. I thought the letters so funny I showed them to my mother. She was appalled at the prospect of her daughter going off to marry an Italian, though I was never going to do anything of the kind. I did not see another letter from Mario, though I'm sure he kept writing. I suspect mother intercepted the letters and destroyed them to protect me.

I started working as a waitress for my father, which cut out the daily travelling and gave me time to take part in plays put on by local amateur dramatic groups, and have elocution lessons once a week.

I still have some of the programmes from our amateur productions. I'm credited with playing Clara Packer in *Mystery at Green Fingers* by J. B. Priestley, 'a comedy of detection in three acts', performed by the Doric Players at the YWCA Centre, Acton. The same group and venue saw me as Anne in *Mr Pim Passed By*, a three act comedy by A. A. Milne. I also appeared as Mary Haddon in *Young Mrs Barrington* by Warren Chester Strode; as Prudence in *Midnight Melodrama* by Vera I. Arlett; as Mrs Noakes in *Birds of Passage* by F. Lefebre.

We'd be performing one play while rehearsing for the next. It was hard work and great fun and I was convinced I was going to claw my way to stardom like all my favourite screen stars: Joan Crawford, Bette Davis, Barbara Stanwyck, Clark Gable, Spencer Tracey, Frederic March.

I went to the cinema as often as I could, memorising lines from my favourite films. So screen-struck was I that on Saturdays I'd go to see one film then run round the corner to another cinema to catch a second.

I was equally enthralled by the cycle of plays at the New Theatre, starring Laurence Olivier and Ralph Richardson. But this time I, too, had learned how to project my voice, how to stand, how to hold my head, the whole craft of acting, but there was a big obstacle to my ever achieving stage success – my looks.

Every time I came on stage, even if I was dressed in character as, say, a maid, there'd be surprised comments from the audience and perhaps a few titters. My unmistakable resemblance to Princess Elizabeth was wrecking any chance I had of sustaining a successful theatrical illusion.

I had hoped my resemblance to the heir of the throne would wear off as I grew older but it didn't. In fact, as the years passed by we became more and more alike.

Like most families in Britain, we got our first television set in 1953 to watch the glorious spectacle of the Coronation, and I moved effortlessly from being the lookalike of Princess Elizabeth to that of Her Majesty Queen Elizabeth II.

Shortly after the Coronation, I went with a friend to a gallery in the centre of London to see the now famous full-length painting of the young Queen in the uniform of the Order of the Garter, newly completed by the Italian portraitist, Pietro Annigoni. We went downstairs to the viewing room and stood back to get a better view of the painting, placing ourselves directly in line with it. I heard someone say, 'Ssh, that looks like the Queen. Be quiet!' I looked at my friend, and we both smiled.

A team of examiners from the Royal Academy of Dramatic Art came up to audition me and other young thespian hopefuls at a little theatre in Ealing. I read my piece, which I had learned fluently, and must have impressed them because I was told I could gain a RADA scholarship.

I was so grateful to my elocution teacher, who had helped prepare me for the examination. Despite my nerves, I had done well, so desperately did I want to train as a professional actress. But the cold reality hit me when I spoke to my parents. They definitely did not want me to go on the stage, and made it clear they could not afford to pay my way while I trained and worked my way into the profession. So, it was not to be. And I had begun to wonder if the struggle to succeed in what must be the most hazardous profession in the world would be worth the effort if I could not overcome my greatest drawback, that likeness to the Queen. I knew my appearance was unlikely to change, so I made the agonising decision to turn down the scholarship and set my sights on another course – emigration. I chose America quite simply because it was a long way off, and people spoke English there. I went to an agency where I fixed myself up with a job as a nanny with a family in Texas. My parents were horrified and tried to talk me out of it. But I was determined to go.

As it turned out, even distance brought no escape from 'recognition'. I travelled across the Atlantic on the Holland American Line's *SS Maasdam* steerage class, but in no time one of the crew came up to me to say the Captain wanted me to join him in first class at the Captain's Table for dinner.

'Why me?' I asked.

'Because you look so much like the Queen,' came the frank reply.

'Here we go again,' I thought. But the Captain's Table was the place the elite met to eat, and steerage class was pervaded with the smell of diesel oil. I couldn't resist the chance of a change of scene so I started eating at the Captain's Table. For the first time I knew what it must feel like to be a queen. Aboard the *Maasdam* I was certainly treated like one. I was given kid-glove treatment, looked after with the utmost courtesy and deference. Lovely! I was invited back again and again – I think I could have dined there every night, but I'd made friends amongst my compatriots in steerage, and I decided to spend time with them. After all, I had to sleep down there.

However, I was not a complete martyr to friendship. The trip lasted for something like ten or twelve days, and I ate at the Captain's Table three or four times. I was caught between delight and embarrassment. I could see people on other tables peering surreptitiously at me, and the rest of the Captain's guests used to talk to each other about me rather than addressing me direct. I felt I was on show all the time. I was much younger than the other guests and not nearly as self-assured. It was an uphill struggle trying to make conversation with a crowd I didn't have much in common with, but fun in its way. The excellent food I ate with the Captain's guests went a long way towards compensating me for any awkwardness I felt there.

In the rest of the ship, too, I'd have different people coming up to me and saying things like, 'You're the star attraction here, aren't you?' I didn't feel it, but it was flattering to be told I was and I got to make friends more easily because of it. It was a long crossing but a thoroughly enjoyable one.

Once ashore I headed for Midland, Texas, a place which was typical of small town America in the mid 1950s. I was to work there as an *au pair*, helping to care for three children of a family in the oil business, as was just about everybody else in the town. Shortly after I arrived, I was doing the washing up in the kitchen when the man of the house said the familiar words, 'Say, Jeannette, do you know you look just like the Queen Elizabeth?'

It soon became a standing joke in the family, and I was quickly in demand locally as an expert on all things British, especially our royalty, for all the news they got in Midland centred on the town itself. I might have been a visiting Martian to them, people were so fascinated with any tit-bits of information I could give them.

A lot of them still thought of England as the Old Country, and wanted to know how people lived there now, the type of houses we had, that sort of thing. There was a great divide between American and British living standards in those days, and it was my introduction to a nation of two-car families.

Information on our royalty was particularly in demand, although they were sometimes dismissed as strange relics of history. My audience was hungry for any tit-bits I could offer them culled from newspapers I'd read at home, but my listeners obviously felt that they were hearing authentic gossip from the royal fireside.

I was slim, had my hair done nicely, and dressed well which tended to make people more aware of my likeness to royalty. Although eager to hear any stories I could tell them, I found that people in the town would say they didn't care about royalty. They would argue that the royal family cost too much money, and what use were they anyway? They'd nod at me and say, 'You look like the Queen of England, but so what? Is she so important?'

It was all an act of course. In fact the Americans I met were awed by the thought of royalty, and jealous that we had such a family and they did not. The people I lived with, for instance, often used to have friends round for the evening. They'd be drinking late into the night and my employer used to get me to serve his guests. In his eyes, it was like having a member of the royal family to wait on them.

I knew I was being used as a showpiece. Some of the other people I met, and they were usually quite wealthy, would invite me to their homes for little soirées. I had no illusions as to why they should have singled out an insignificant *au pair*. I was there as a figure of amusement, of entertainment – 'their' Queen. They wanted me at their dinner table to impress their friends. I found myself talking until all hours of the night about our royal family, why we had one, what use they were, and all that sort of thing. It got a bit boring after a while, but I didn't really mind. If I had, I would have not been party to it. I was a long way from home, and it was pleasant to be made a fuss of, to be able to eat and drink in such style.

On the evenings I was free from this demanding social round, I would go to the village hall to take part in theatrical readings with members of the local repertory group, strictly for the fun of it now that my acting ambitions were over. I also joined a club, I think it was called The Overseas Club, which consisted mainly of German and Italian girls, GI brides, who had come to America after the war. They, too, would spot my likeness to the Queen and make good-natured jokes about it.

When I completed my year's contract as an *au pair*, I decided to stay in Midland and take a job with an oil company as a shorthand typist. I had acquired secretarial skills back in Wembley on the nights I was not treading the theatrical boards and they came in very useful now. My resemblance to the Queen was remarked on in my new job, and had the decided advantage of attracting a lot of boyfriends from among the company's employees.

Midland was a dusty town in the area of Texas known as the Panhandle, right in the middle of sagebrush country, and a high spot on dates was being taken over the Rio Grande to Juarez, the first town across the Mexican border. The incredible and sudden contrast between the wealth of America and the poverty of Mexico was always a shock.

Then one day Ken Charles drove into town from an oil rig he had been working on. He was covered in the dust and grime of an oil drilling site, and looked like some kind of refugee.

He strode into a local bank and a counter clerk said to him, 'You must be English.'

'How do you know?' Ken asked.

'Because you're the only person in town without pressed pants.'

Ken wanted to cash some sterling traveller's cheques, but this out of the way bank had never seen them so he had to wait around while telephone calls were made. While he was waiting, the clerk, who happened to know me, started chatting to him.

'Are you single?' the matchmaker asked. When he learned Ken was he told him, 'We've got a very nice English girl here in town, and she's a bit homesick. Funny thing, she looks just like your Queen. I'm sure she'd like to meet you.'

And that's how I received a telephone call out of the blue with a lovely English voice asking me, 'How would you like to come out with me tonight?'

I rang the clerk and asked if the man looked respectable.

'Sure he's respectable, though he looks a bit dirty,' he said. 'If I had a daughter I'd let her go out with him.'

So Ken and I went to dinner that night, and I found out he worked for British Petroleum and was making a tour of America, meeting oil company executives, before going up to Calgary in Canada.

He was in Midland for a week, and we saw each other every night. Ken chuckled over my likeness to the Queen, but didn't give any further thought to it. I suppose that was one of the reasons I liked him. We fell for each other immediately. Ken had to go off to Calgary, thousands of miles away from Midland, but we kept in touch. It was, however, too much of a strain carrying out a proper courtship long-distance, so I followed him to Canada and got a job there. We were married in Calgary in 1957 but I'll always remember Midland with the most affection, the town that brought me such a wonderful husband.

Ken's family, in fact, originated only a few miles away from mine. How strange that we had to go all that way to find each other. We still visit Midland when we take holidays in America, and some of the people I met there are great friends of ours to this day.

Calgary was the cattle capital of the state of Alberta, way out west, freezing cold in winter and burning hot in summer. Its days as a new frontier oil boom town were still some years off. It's not much of an exaggeration to say that in 1957 nothing happened there. Ken went to work overseeing drilling operations, and I settled down to being a housewife and then a mother when our first son, David, was born. People would still remark on my similarity to the Queen, though because I didn't visit the hairdresser's so often and didn't dress up as much as I used to, the number of recognitions seemed to be diminishing.

Oddly enough, I caught my first 'live' sight of the Queen in the backwoods of Canada, when she and Prince Philip arrived as guests at the Calgary Stampede, a cow town spectacle like nothing else on earth. Ken and I also watched the Stampede and drew remarks like, 'Are you having a walkabout?'

It was when I ventured out of Canada that the old double trouble recurred. Once I was travelling in a taxi through Brooklyn, where I was visiting a friend, when the driver asked me for my autograph. I asked why. He said, 'Come on, I know who you are.' He passed me a piece of paper and I signed, 'Jeannette Charles'. I gave it back to him and he stared at it incredulously. I thought he was going to explode. He gave me another piece of paper and, in a most threatening way, said, "Sign 'Elizabeth'." I did, and he seemed much happier. I felt a little guilty but decidedly safer.

Another time in New York I went with some friends to the famous Jack Dempsey's restaurant on Times Square where we sat in the window to get a good view of the skyscrapers towering above us. The Queen was known to be in the city at the time, and a passer-by stopped to peer in at me when he saw me sitting in the restaurant window. He was joined by another, then another. Soon there was a huge crowd pressed up against the window which looked as if it would break. The crowd got bigger and bigger until eventually it was so huge that, although we hadn't finished our meal, the manager pleaded with us to slip out by a back door to keep his window intact and disperse the throng which was threatening to jam up the square.

On our way to visit my family in England, David and I travelled by

Greyhound Bus from Calgary to New York, where we went to Idlewild (now J. F. Kennedy) Airport to catch a plane to London. I went to one of the airport shops to buy some chocolate for David, but could not get served because all the staff were otherwise engaged, fawning over a little man in a suit of large and very loud checks. He wanted a camera, then after shave, then something else. He had three assistants running around after him and David was starting to yell for his chocolate.

I finally called out to one of the girls: 'Excuse me, would you please let me have a bar of chocolate for my son? That's all I want.'

'Sorry, we're serving this customer,' she replied.

At this the man in front of me turned round, flashed me a charming smile and said: 'Please serve this lady first. Get her the chocolates or whatever it is she wants.' David was looking very appealing in a miniature peaked cap, and my rescuer patted him on the head and said: 'What a lovely little fellow.' I realised I was meeting Sammy Davis Junior, one of the biggest international stars of the day. I was very impressed by his courteous, gentlemanly behaviour.

At that moment, somebody tapped me on the shoulder and I turned to see a press photographer standing behind me.

'Do you want her with me?' Sammy asked, smiling accommodatingly.

'No, thanks. I'd like the lady on her own – she looks so much like the Queen.'

I was mortified! Sammy Davis, a megastar, was being pushed aside while I was photographed, my face as red as a beetroot. When the photographer had finished, I was desperate to get away. 'I've got to go now,' I said. 'I've really got to go.' 'It's been very nice to have met you, ma'am,' Sammy said with a graceful bow, playing up to the royal joke like the trouper he is.

Our second son, Peter, was born on a visit to England where we bought a house in the tranquil Essex village of Danbury, close to Chelmsford. Then we were off to the coffee belt of Colombia, in South America, to live in a company villa on the edge of the jungle in a remote town which gloried under the name of Bucaramanga.

Ken spent most of his time at the drilling site while I was left behind at the house to look after the children and maintain discipline among our Colombian maids. The expatriate colony there was full of stories of maids who stole everything that would move from the house and then skipped off back to their native village. Getting these girls to work was no easy task.

The company's agent, Senor Fernandez, said: 'You've got to keep them in check, or they won't do anything. They won't work, they'll just chatter all day.' Then he spotted a framed photograph of me, which looked very much like the Queen. He took the photograph to show the two girls who had been assigned to me and told them sternly, 'You must do as you are told because you are working for a very important lady. She is one of her country's ruling family.'

It worked like a charm. I had absolutely no trouble with the girls from that moment, although I spoke no Spanish. I'd often see them staring at the photograph, then at me.

Next stop for the travelling Charles family was Libya, the oil-rich desert state in North Africa then ruled by King Idris. Our houseboy, who used to work on the British Army base there, always called me 'My Queen' because he said I looked so like the royal portraits he had seen at the barracks. He was a very nice man, and always looked after us well. Our daughter, Carol, was born in the British Military Hospital at Benghazi which means she is also a Libyan citizen. This was brought home to us recently when she received her call-up papers for the Libyan Army. What a thought, my daughter being drilled by one of Gadaffi's instructors!

The political unrest which signalled the end of King Idris' rule began in the mid-1960s when it was considered prudent for us to return to England. Ken became Drilling Manager for British Petroleum, based at their headquarters in London, and we settled down in Danbury.

At home in the village I was 'recognised' very rarely but I found that when I ventured further afield, the familiar problem would recur. I'd be out with a friend, hear the whispering around us and walk briskly on, praying there wouldn't be a sudden delighted outburst of 'That's the Queen'. I didn't always get away with it. Often someone would come up to me and say something like 'Oh, you do look like the Queen. Did you know that?' It could spoil the day out for me and for any friend who happened to be with me.

The West End of London was always the worst place for being sighted. In the Oxford Street Marks and Spencer I was looking through some clothes with my face carefully averted when I noticed a little girl staring intently up at me. She shouted, very loudly, 'Mummy, there's the Queen!'

I just wanted to hide. I could sense heads being turned to look in our direction. There was nothing else for it – I ran.

On another occasion I had been visiting some American friends at the Hilton Hotel in Park Lane when a girl walked up to me in the lobby, bobbed a neat curtsey, and said, 'Excuse me, ma'am, would you please have a look at this, and perhaps you can help us.' She handed me a leaflet about the homeless. I blushed scarlet, feeling dreadfully guilty, and scooted for home as fast as I could.

Even travelling by train was fraught with hazards. I was with Ken one morning, headed for Liverpool Street, when a woman came up to me and said, 'You know, you're incredibly like the Queen.' A whole carriageful of people mutely confirmed that I was, then carried on reading their papers.

After a few encounters like this, I started wearing hats and keeping my face averted as I walked down unfamiliar streets. It was neither easy nor pleasant and I found myself becoming increasingly wary of entering crowds of people, fearing that one person might 'recognise' me and then I'd be trapped.

Some cases of mistaken identity could work to my advantage, though. I'd turn up at clubs or restaurants with my husband or a friend and the staff would make a great deal of fuss of me and always lead me to best table. We'd get assiduous service from a whole bevy of waiters and waitresses, all intent on examining me at close quarters.

Of course, there have been moments when the Queen has been mistaken for me. Take the Christmas Day television broadcasts to the Commonwealth, for instance. When my children were very young they would jump up and down as the Queen's face appeared on the television screen, shouting, 'Look! There's Mummy!'

My most traumatic moment of recognition ever came in a face to face encounter with the Queen.

I'd heard that Her Majesty was to visit the nearby town of Maldon to honour its 800th anniversary celebrations, and that her route there would take her through my village, along the main road at the end of my street. So, at the time she was expected, around two in the afternoon, I left my home and walked up the hill with a friend to take up a position on the main road. There weren't many people there so there was no question of our having to battle for a place.

After a little while we heard a few scattered cheers as the royal car drove slowly through the outskirts of the village then we, too, caught sight of the royal Rolls-Royce, gleaming in the sunlight. I remember wondering what on earth they do to their vehicles to make them sparkle so. Slowly, the car glided past the village's war memorial. I could see the figure of the Queen inside what appeared to be a cockpit of glass. She was wearing a beautiful yellow dress and looked wonderful. Then the car drew alongside me. I was standing right to the edge of the kerb, close enough to the car to have been able to reach out and touch it. The Queen inclined her head, waving gently all the time, glanced in my direction – and froze, staring, hand immobile in the air as our eyes met from a distance of a couple of feet. In fact, the car was so close it almost brushed against me.

As it moved on, she turned her head to keep me in sight. I stood transfixed. The Queen was looking out of the rear window as the car went up a slight incline. She was still staring after me as the car reached a bend in the road and slid out of sight. I watched her receding, powerless to move. Even when she had gone, I stood staring at the empty road. It was as if I was paralysed.

I had known for years that we were very similar in looks but when I saw her at close quarters that day it was as if I had stared into a mirror. The living proof was too much for me. I started shaking like a jelly, and could feel tears welling up in my eyes. I felt dizzy and sick, and thought I was going to pass out.

There are those who believe that everyone has a double somewhere in the world, and who can say? Maybe it's true. What I do know is that when you see your *doppelganger*, the effect is cataclysmic.

I tottered home, sat down, trembling, cried. It took me a long time to recover enough to make a cup of tea.

The Queen had looked stunned, too. If the sighting affected her as it affected me, she must have felt shattered.

This is the only time we have met face to face, and I never want to go through that experience again. Without meaning to be ungracious, once is enough for me, it was just too much of a shock.

CHAPTER THREE

My Second Career

The misunderstanding over my portrait, which brought me to the attention of the world's press, happened in the summer of 1972. The tidal wave of interest in Mrs Jeannette Charles, housewife, would be shortlived I was sure but I rather wanted to take advantage of it while it lasted.

When David Thurlow, the *Daily Express* reporter who had started the ball rolling, called me again, I asked him to arrange something. I knew that some filming was taking place at the EMI studios at Elstree, and asked if he would take me there to watch it going on. I'd always wanted to see a film set in action, and I thought I'd cash in on my bit of fame, however fleeting, to fulfil that particular ambition.

David said he would be delighted, and that he might also do a story about my visit. So that was how I came to be escorted into the studios and on to the set of 'The Best Pair of Legs in the World', a film starring Reg Varney. As I came into view, every member of the cast and studio staff froze. Reg Varney wasn't sure what to think until he was introduced to me, then he chuckled and said, 'You certainly had us fooled. We thought the Queen was making a surprise visit.' I asked for his autograph and he said, 'I've heard about you, and I wish you the best of luck.' I was going to need it.

Shortly after this I was invited up to Thames Television in London to appear on their early evening local news show. In the green room, where guests relax before appearing in front of the cameras, I met a diminutive Italian photographer, Raymond Bellisarrio. Mr Bellisarrio has earned himself a great deal of notoriety, and, I believe, a sizeable income, by taking long focus 'candid' photographs of our royal family. He will track them everywhere, waiting for those unguarded, unflattering moments he delights in capturing on film. Mr Bellisarrio is a renowned member of that peculiarly Italian breed, the *papparazzi*, literally 'pests'. He may well be pestilential to the royals but he possesses a great deal of charm in his dealings with commoners.

I approached him in the green room and asked him, 'Can you tell me what it is about me that is *not* like the Queen?'

He stood back to view me expertly then said, 'Well, you're a little shorter than her but that shouldn't be any problem to you. If you carry on this business, you should always wear high heels. The Queen wears irridescent make-up, which is made especially for her and the other ladies of the royal family. You probably won't be able to get that, but if you aim for a pink and white colouring, you'll look good. As you know, I'm very familiar with the royal family, and I think you should do well.'

'Doing what?' I asked.

'You could do modelling, or more appearances on chat shows. You never know with television. You may be asked all over the world after this one airing.'

I had not set out to impersonate the Queen. Although the similarity between us had been part of my life for many years it had never occurred to me that I might be able to use it. Now, unexpectedly, word of the resemblance between us had reached journalists as far afield as South America and Australia. They came to interview me and photograph me doing things around the home, working in my garden or walking around the streets. If hard-bitten journalists were so fascinated, no wonder that other people, too, were beginning to take an interest in me. I was about to begin my second career.

During those early days I got a call from someone locally who wanted me to open up a grocer's shop and sign some photographs of myself. I agreed to do this, and spent a really lovely day. The people who came into the shop were fascinated by me, particularly the children. None of them had ever had the opportunity of meeting the Queen. If the nearest they could get to it was to encounter someone who looked like her, that was good enough for them. At the end of the day I told the shop owner that the prints I had given out had cost me £5 and she reimbursed me. That was all the money I got from her but by the time the story found its way into a newspaper, a fertile imagination had boosted the £5 expenses into a fee of £500, and the headlines on the story screeched 'What a cheek this woman has!'

I was very upset and tried to make the truth known but no one was interested in publishing the mundane facts.

I started to see that a lot of newspapers and magazines were profiting from my accidental resemblance to a figure of world renown. Photographs of me, too, were now syndicated world-wide yet the one person making nothing out of them was me.

'If they can make money out of photographing me, why shouldn't I get some of it myself?' I thought.

I'd also reached the stage where I found I had time on my hands. My two sons were away at boarding school and, although I adore my home and looking after it and my family, I didn't relish the idea of spending the rest of my life pottering about within its confines.

A number of agencies had written to me, asking if I would like to go on their books, and I selected one whose letter impressed me. The Ugly Agency had been in existence for about a year, and had been set up by three photographers who had spotted a demand for an agency supplying models who could fill out the spots in advertisements where glamour was not required. Taxi drivers and housewives could join this agency. So did I and, predictably, the press had a field day. I recall one newspaper heading reading 'Queen's double is an official Ugly'. As one of the girls who ran the agency explained, 'Though we handle two hundred models under the Ugly title, they are really just faces with character. Certainly, Mrs Charles is not ugly, any more than the Queen is.'

Strangely my first advertising assignments had nothing to do with my most natural attributes. I appeared in a television commercial for cigars which became famous as a sort of silent comedy classic in its field. In it, Jeremy Childs walks out of a beer parlour wearing a huge, wide-brimmed hat. It is raining, and he lights up a long cigar which stretches right to the brim of the hat but is protected from the rain. My part involved rushing past with a man, both of us shielded under an umbrella. The advertisement was shown widely and received great acclaim in the world of advertising but my part in it passed almost unnoticed.

Then there was the beer commercial in which I appeared as a waitress, another in which I wore a boiler suit, and a magazine spread featuring an electric blanket in which, wearing dressing gown and curlers, I took part in a line up of fairly dowdy housewives. I will certainly never forget the advertisement in which some of the detergent got into my eyes.

'Sorry about that, Jeannette,' said the girl in charge briskly. 'Now we'll have to do another shot.' It was my first taste of 'the show must go on'.

My second career was taking its first faltering steps when I was chosen to be the photographic model for a *London Weekly Advertiser* poster destined for display in the capital's underground stations. I was told to wear an ordinary summer dress and to go to Brown's Hotel in the West End of London. They sat me in an ornate chair against some old wood-panelling, a graceful table to one side of me. The finishing touch was the stuffed corgi they placed at my feet. I was given a copy of the *London Weekly Advertiser* to hold open, as if I were reading it. The paper specialises in property advertisements, and two lines of copy at the bottom of the finished poster read, 'If your home no longer meets your needs, then why not look in the *London Weekly Advertiser*?' It was to be displayed on hoardings throughout the underground system and I was proud to feature so prominently in a large, beautifully produced poster. I still have a copy of it among my souvenirs.

However, London's travelling public were denied the pleasure of enjoying the joke. The London Transport Executive rejected the poster because, according to their commercial advertisement officer, 'We feel it is in very bad taste. We regard it as insulting to the royal family.' The advertising agency which dreamed up the idea said they considered the poster amusing and lighthearted and did not believe it would cause offence. Jill Searle of the Ugly Agency was amazed by the ban. 'I'm sure if Prince Philip saw it, he would die laughing,' she told me. 'Both he and the Queen have a tremendous sense of humour. And, anyway, nobody could possibly mistake it for the Queen.' The photographer who took the picture for the poster told me he thought the corgi at my feet caused all the trouble.

I was heartbroken by the ban. I cried and cried. Certainly my photograph on the poster had borne an uncanny resemblance to the Queen which was what made it such an eyecatcher, but no one was going to believe the Queen herself had posed for an advertisement. They would know it was a model.

Nevertheless, the poster was banned and I thought I was destined for an ignominious end also. 'That's it,' I thought. 'I'm finished. That's the end for me, before I've even really got started.'

Nothing could have been further from the truth. Sure the newspapers chorused 'Stop ridiculing the Queen!' and 'Abdicate!' but the more noise they made, the more controversy they drummed up, the more exposure I was getting. Publicity over the poster ban followed that surrounding Jane Thornhill's portrait of me. The journalists were once again beating a path to my door, and advertisers abroad were taking note.

One such were the bottler's of a Scotch whisky sold in Italy under the brand name Francis. I flew out to Milan, where I had some first-hand experience of the *papparazzi* on their home ground. If I had not been through it myself, I would not believe descriptions of it. The photographers were all over me on the coach which took passengers from the airplane to the terminal, and they plagued me all the way to the taxi rank. They smothered me like an army of ants, practically photographing up my nostrils, leaving me feeling awkward and distressed.

A studio had been made ready for my photo session. A mock window gave onto a backdrop of a London street scene. Inside the room set, a display cabinet contained a couple of strategically-placed crowns. I sat at an elegant table, a glass of what was in fact cold tea in my hand – apparently it photographs as whisky better than the real stuff – a bottle of Francis whisky beside me on the table.

It made a beautiful poster and was in no way undignified but somehow word of its existence reached the office of the Lord Chamberlain in England, and a stiff letter was sent to the Scottish distillers who supply Francis. The letter described the campaign as offensive, and warned that it could be punishable in this country. Newspapers joined the attack. 'Lay off our royal family!' bellowed one headline. Here we go again . . .

The owner of the Francis firm, Signor Francesco Angelini, protested: 'It is absolutely not offensive. It was done with a typical English sense of humour. It's a fun thing. I would not be offended if a Scotch Whisky firm in Britain used the figure of the Italian President in its advertising.'

Wrong Mac. The Scottish distillers said they would not supply Francis with any more whisky unless the advertising campaign was called off. It was, but Signor Angelini had the last laugh. Because of the controversy and the resultant publicity, sales of his whisky went up.

It was all so silly. The royal family are used to having jokes made about them on radio and television – good, healthy jokes – and they don't let it worry them. I think this sort of thing happens because people around royalty get over-protective, and by the time word reaches the family, they can't very well step forward and say they don't mind.

Of course, if the whisky had been made in Italy, nothing could have been done. As it was, the agency in Milan called me up to say they were very sorry but that they had no option but to withdraw. That, as they say, is showbusiness.

Controversy was clearly going to be a close companion, and one I would have to get used to for I was not going to give up modelling because of a few alarmist cries of outrage, and short of having plastic surgery or wearing a mask, I would always be mistaken for the Queen.

Controversy was waiting in the wings when I made my first appearance at the London Palladium.

The telephone rang at home and I answered it to find myself speaking to Dorothy Squires.

'I want you at my show, dressed as the Queen,' she said. 'Can you do it?'

I've been an admirer of Dorothy's for as long as I remember. She's always been a marvellous singer and performer, and I felt honoured to be asked. This engagement was for one of her periodic London Palladium shows, when she would book the theatre herself and play to a packed audience of delighted fans.

When I arrived at the Palladium, I was shown into the green room and moments later Dorothy came in to greet me like a long lost friend. 'I'm delighted you've come tonight because you're going to make my show for me,' she told me.

It was a really dazzling evening, and my entrance was beautifully staged. The main lights were dimmed and a spotlight trained on the royal box which is set just above stage level. Then, dressed as the Queen in the full regalia of evening gown, sash and tiara, I stepped forward into the box as the National Anthem was played.

During the first half of the show, a comedian started up a little banter with me, asking for a particular card. I had a giant pack of playing cards with me and threw out the one he requested. It was harmless fun.

When Dorothy came on to perform, she gave me a wave and raised a cheer for 'Her Majesty'. During her act, she made further references to 'Her Majesty'. It was all a wonderful spoof which the audience loved. Dorothy herself was so marvellous, a real star, but she troubled to call me up later to say 'Thank you very much for your wonderful performance.' It was a memorable show and I still meet people who say 'I was there that night', and talk fondly about it.

Not so memorable was the barb delivered by gossip columnist Nigel

Dempster, who labelled my performance 'An example of extreme bad taste'. Oh well, Mr Dempster, if you must take it so seriously!

Despite this criticism, the appearance was a great boost for me and I later attended another of Dorothy's Palladium shows when I sat in the stalls and was introduced to the audience along with celebrity guests like David Jansen and Raquel Welch. However, when the Darts pop group wanted me to appear in the royal box at one of their Palladium concerts, the plan was squelched by the theatre's management. Dorothy could do as she wished on the nights she took over the Palladium but the pop group was there on a night for which the management were responsible. The manager, John Avery, very politely rang me up to reassure me: 'It has nothing to do with your professional expertise, it's just that we don't think it would be right.'

So my lookalike career was firmly on the road, and marking out a path which others would follow. I have been acknowledged as the first of the lookalikes, and the person who put them on the map, particularly the royal carbon copies. Even impressionists have developed a royal repertoire now. Mike Yarwood, for example, started impersonating Prince Charles shortly after I came on the scene.

In fact, I remember when the word 'lookalike' entered the vocabulary. I was being interviewed by a journalist, who said, 'Now, you're the double of the Queen.'

'Please don't say I'm her double,' I corrected him. 'I am mistaken for the Queen, and have always been mistaken for her, but I'm shorter and a little fatter – hardly her double.'

'Well, you look extremely like her, and some angles are perfect,' he said. 'You're a sort of lookalike . . .'

'Yes, that's the word,' I said. 'Use it. It's wonderful.'

'I don't think it's been used before,' the journalist said – a rare event in the world of newspapers. 'It will look good in headlines.'

I made a television appearance on an afternoon chat show with Mavis Nicholson, seated behind a cloth and visible only in silhouette. The cloth was suddenly whipped away, and we could hear the audience draw in a collective breath as they thought they recognised the Queen.

I also appeared with Russell Harty on his show, Russell Harty Plus, and had to come on after Fenella Fielding, which was quite an act to follow. I was a bit confused on that occasion. With a sizeable live audience in the studio, I wasn't sure whether to address myself to them or to Russell. But I need not have worried. He was so friendly and courteous and helpful it was easy to be just naturally myself. I stopped worrying about the people watching at home, the critics, the relatives who would know if I didn't tell the truth, my friends and what they might think of my notoriety.

Russell told me that my appearance on his show sparked off an idea to put together a book containing some of his most interesting interviews. We had photographs taken drinking tea together for *TV Times* publicity, and they came out so well that Russell wanted to use one of the pictures for the cover of his book. This idea was rejected because the photograph of me looked just too much like the Queen, and it was feared it might smack of misrepresentation. When they wanted to use the picture in *The Bookseller*, the weekly bible of the book trade, it was turned down for the same reason. Royal dignity was maintained by finding a home for that photograph on the endpapers of Russell's book. It's nice to see it there, and a reminder of those early exciting days.

I was soon a regular on television shows around the country as everybody seemed to want to know what it felt like to be mistaken for the Queen. I rarely used props in those days – such as pearls, clothing, hairswitches and so on – and I remember when Thames Television asked me to come back to be interviewed by Eamonn Andrews they said they wanted me to dress up for the appearance in hat, coat and gloves, and drive to the studios in a Rolls-Royce. I was escorted inside in regal style and it felt marvellous, something I could definitely get used to. Eamonn was such fun to talk to. He's a gorgeous interviewer, very direct, and he is not interested in trying to worm something out of you that you might regret having said. I thoroughly enjoyed our conversation, and the audience appreciated the royal charade.

The complaints about my early advertising ventures failed to scare off a company who wanted me in a promotional film about their silver polish. I was then photographed astride a motorbike with a corgi at my feet, for a motorcycle magazine, and a company which manufactures disposable plates commissioned a magazine advertisement which depicts me seated on a gilded chair, eating a meal off one of their plates. Largely, though, companies in this country have tended to avoid using me in advertisements, probably because they fear some unwelcome intervention in their campaign. Some, bolder than the rest, like pop groups, have used me for record covers but apart from these and the few campaigns I've described, most of my advertising work has been carried out abroad, notably in Germany, where, for some reason that totally escapes me, the population is fascinated by our royal family.

CHAPTER FOUR

‘Get the woman who looks like the Queen’

When I was offered a spot on a Christmas edition of 'Who Do You Do?' I told the producer that if I didn't consider the sketch in good taste, I'd get up and walk out. Brave words from a newcomer, you might think, but nothing could persuade me to take part in anything which I thought was insulting to Her Majesty. I am a staunch royalist and I would hate to be part of anything that upset or embarrassed our royal family in any way.

I need not have worried; my scene was just plain funny. The television wardrobe department supplied me with queenly regalia and I joined the cast of a show which, as its name implies, consists of people doing impressions. The others in the show were, like me, new faces on television, and they have all gone on to bigger and better things. Freddie Starr and Jim Davidson were just two of the now familiar faces.

My part called for me to stand stock still while one of the cast spoke to me in a respectful manner and another ran a wriggling model snake up and down my back. I managed to keep a straight face though it was not at all easy.

The show was a memorable one, and even now I find people refer to it in conversation with me. I felt privileged to have taken part, and looked forward to further variety appearances on television.

Afterwards, Freddie Starr brought his wife, who was expecting a baby, to my dressing room and they stayed for a chat. This sort of friendliness and acceptance of me as a fellow professional is what has impressed me most about the showbusiness people with whom I have worked. They have been almost uniformly kind to a raw beginner, welcoming me with open arms.

I vividly recall, for example, bumping into that fabulous comedian, Dick Emery, in a television studio canteen.

'You've got on very well, haven't you?' he said to me encouragingly.

Ever eager to learn what I could about my new profession, I asked, 'Can you give me any advice?'

He rolled his eyes and said in his campest voice: 'As queens go, I don't think you need any.'

We both had a good chuckle about this, because within his repertoire was a famous drag queen, Mandy.

Faith Brown, the brilliant impression artist whose *pièce de résistance* is her superb Margaret Thatcher, has often said to me, 'I wish I had your face – not your body, I don't want your body – just your face!'

Perhaps the most innovative comic genius of our time is Spike Milligan, and his fertile mind has conjured up many ways to use me in his television shows. He made his demands plain in a note he wrote to one of his staff which I still have in my possession. The note read simply, 'Get the woman who looks like the Queen.'

I appeared throughout the latter half of his 'Q' series. In my first sketch I was seated on a chair in profile before a white screen; my head looked like the stamp upon a plain envelope. At a hand signal, I was to press a button by my side, triggering a mechanism like an ejector seat which threw me off-screen. Like most visual jokes it doesn't sound much but it looked very funny on screen. Spike seemed delighted, and the crew gave me a big round of applause, making me feel very much at home.

Spike was always so busy writing or performing that he didn't seem to have time to give out stage directions; it was as if he expected things to happen naturally. Perhaps that's the secret of his magic. He was always very friendly to me and used to call me 'Your Maj', with a little bow for I was always dressed in queenly regalia for my regular spots with him.

In a later 'Q' scene, with Spike dressed as a tramp hanging about outside Buckingham Palace, I had to walk past him, hear him say something in gobbledygook which I obviously didn't like, take a gun from my handbag and shoot him. It sounds crazy but it was very funny on screen. For another sketch I was walking along in regal manner with a courtier by my side when Spike approached me. Without breaking my stride I picked up a huge lemon meringue pie and slapped it into his face. (I must admit I didn't enjoy doing this so much because I had the sneaking suspicion he just might slap me back. He didn't, fortunately.) I also appeared in a cameo as the Queen on a facsimile of a pound note, and in a garden party sequence a ball was lobbed over a wall to land in a glass of wine I was holding. We then went on location to a country spot to film me dressed as the Queen with a 'Prince Philip' by my side, both of us walking about with trumpets on our heads and Spike with us wearing a pair of disreputable shorts. God knows what the locals must have thought.

I also appeared with Spike in a television show called 'The Melting Pot'. He played an Indian lift man in a place that was supposed to resemble the top people's store. I walked into the lift and he jumped up and down, shouting, 'It's Her Maj! It's Her Maj!'

Of course, Spike does know how to behave with genuine royalty. He confided to me with great seriousness during one filming session 'I've met the Queen, you know.'

My introduction to 'The Goodies' involved taking part in a sketch alongside people dressed up as Dracula, Kojak (complete with lollipop), Colombo, and The Devil. I was supplied with the full queenly regalia, including tiara, and we stood in line as a series of mock waxwork exhibits. It was the sort of unexpected scene which made 'The Goodies' such a popular show. But on a later occasion their particular brand of zany humour almost drowned me.

We were filming a washed out garden party sketch at the Ruislip Lido, which is more like a great river than a swimming pool. The Goodies themselves had rowed out into the middle while I was fitted out in a wet suit topped with a beautiful gown, gloves and, of course, a tiara. I felt about twice my normal size and totally ridiculous. I was given a velvet cushion with a row of medals on it and told to walk out to The Goodies, who were waiting in their rowing boat.

'Go!' the director ordered, and I started walking very slowly into the water, wobbling on my high heels as I went. The water passed my knees, then my waist. On and on I went, as the water mounted higher and higher so did my hysteria. I can't swim!

'I can't back out now', I thought. 'If I do I'll lose the job, I'll get a bad reputation, and I won't work again.'

My skirts started to float around me, obstructing my view. I was up to my neck in water, feeling sick and panic-stricken, and still the director was shouting through his megaphone: 'Come on, Jeannette, keep going! That's right, Jeannette, don't worry about a thing.'

We'd started filming late, it was about seven o'clock at night by now and darkness was falling. I felt my stiletto heels sinking into the mud and started to keel over, then a hand took hold of one of my arms. It seemed I would either drown or fall victim to the monster of Ruislip Lido but I didn't much care, I felt so cold and miserable. Then I spotted a frogman peering at me through his mask. He was saying something to me but I couldn't make it out. It sounded like gobbledygook, and I wondered if it was all part of the show.

Finally I distinguished: 'Don't worry, Jeannette, I'm here to protect you.'

The director called impatiently, 'Come on now, Jeannette, a little quicker.'

'Any further and I'll drown,' I thought. Didn't they care about their Queen – nobody had even checked if I could swim! My nerve snapped. I was going to disobey a director's order. 'I can't go any further,' I said. 'I can't swim!' And then, up to my neck in water, I started to cry.

I heard the exasperated director say, 'Oh, God, now she tells us!'

Nimbly, I turned back, heading for shore and, I thought, the end of my career. But they had prepared for this eventuality, it seemed. A stunt girl dressed in gown, gloves, tiara and rubber suit exactly like mine slipped into the water carrying an identical cushion strewn with medals. She went out further than I had dared to then slid beneath the surface. The medals floated on the water, short of the Goodies. The stunt had worked perfectly and was very funny to watch.

The crew at the side of the Lido clapped and cheered as I made my way on to dry land. One said reassuringly, 'You were absolutely marvellous, I don't know where you got the guts from.'

The Goodies came over and said, 'Jeannette, you were great, just great.' Everybody always is in showbusiness circles, of course, but on that occasion I really felt that *I* deserved a medal, let alone The Goodies.

These sketches were fine as far as they went but I was not allowed to speak in any of my television appearances to date because the actors' union, Equity, banned non-members from talking parts. I maintained that I was only there as the Queen's lookalike, and as I alone was uniquely qualified to do so, was not taking work away from another actress.

When that didn't wash I sorted through my belongings to find some treasured, yellowing playbills, souvenirs of my amateur acting appearances with the Doric Players at the Acton YWCA and the 'Ad Astra' group at Ealing. Surely these established my credentials as an experienced actress?

Equity saw it differently. 'She has no professional experience and cannot be allowed to take the bread from the mouths of professionals,' they insisted. They told me that to qualify for union membership I would have to complete forty-two weeks of work. My time with the repertory companies could count towards my qualifying period, they said, as well as any other occasions on which I could prove I'd been working as an actress in television or elsewhere. I wasn't in a long running stage show or even a regular television show so it was going to take a long time for my days and half days of work to amount to forty-two weeks.

I remember going off to Croydon to appear in a charity show there around this time. I was allowed a talking role, a little sketch I had put together myself, because the venue was a theatre where Equity and non-Equity performers could appear together. Top of the bill was a then little-known astrologer called Russell Grant, backed by a bunch of singers and dancers.

Russell and the others liked my performance so much they said they wanted to get a petition together to request Equity to grant me membership. I was touched by this generous thought but would not let them do it as it might have jeopardised their own position.

However, some of the publicity surrounding the charity show came to the attention of John Farrow, a very well-known theatrical producer, who was staging a music hall bill at the Intimate Theatre, Palmers Green.

He rang me up and said, 'I've read about your difficulty in getting an Equity card. One or two of our members have actually worked with you and say you're not bad at all, and they don't see why you shouldn't have one. I'd like to help you.'

'How?' I asked.

'Well, we've got a show called "Musical Medley" coming along,' he said. 'We've got Sandy Powell and his wife, and Lester Ferguson – very well-known names – and there are one or two others. We can't pay you much, but we thought we could help you by putting you in a professional show where you can be seen by any critic, or anybody from Equity or the *Stage* magazine who wants to come along.'

'That sounds very generous,' I said, 'but I really can't sing or dance.'

'Don't worry about that, we'll help you. We can give you tuition because we've got Jenny Hanley as choreographer for the dancers, and she's prepared to give you some training.'

Once again, I was overwhelmed by the friendliness and support of showbusiness people. They didn't know me personally but they were prepared to put themselves out for me like this.

I went along to Jenny Hanley's home and she took me though the Florrie Ford songs they wanted me to sing. I don't have much of a voice, so I had to sing on a very low register. She showed me how to do this and to project my voice at the same time, and she also taught me some dance steps.

John Farrow's idea was to have me dress up in an Edwardian-style dress and be billed as, 'Florrie Ford, Queen of the Music Hall', which was the title that Florrie used to have. It was a good play on words, from lookalike of the Queen of England to lookalike of the queen of the music hall.

I was delighted to be appearing on the same bill as Sandy Powell. Remember him? 'Can you hear me, Mother?' was his catchphrase.

I appeared for three nights, and sang old favourites like 'Walking on the Promenade', 'After the Ball', and 'Hello, hello, who's your lady friend?' I also danced a bit. The audience were great, clapping and cheering my efforts and really giving their support but I know I wasn't very good. In fact, I'm sure I was absolutely atrocious. Luckily, it wasn't my singing and dancing that the theatre was primarily after. They wanted the publicity from my being there, and they got that.

My daughter, Carol, sat through all the shows, bless her, to give me a bit of moral support. An Equity representative was also there for the first night, but what he thought about it has gone unrecorded, thankfully.

There was talk at the time that I might be asked to appear in an coming pantomime with Tony Blackburn, who was then at the height of his popularity. He came along to the Intimate Theatre with his wife, Tessa Wyatt, but I never got the invitation to join him on the boards. Perhaps he had seen enough!

I persisted with my stage and television work, slowly clocking up my appearance time over the next couple of years until finally I got my Equity card. What a day that was! I felt I was really established at last. I took a bottle of champagne up to my agent's office and we drank it together to celebrate a great moment in my life.

The first speaking role I got was in the television series 'Mind Your

Language' in which I played a woman who visits a college looking for her husband, only to be mistaken for the Queen by some of the language students there. As I'm very familiar with cases of mistaken identity, I felt quite at home in the role.

The menace of water followed me when I became a regular in 'The Rutles', a series which Eric Idle, formerly of the Monty Python team, developed for BBC2. One sketch was shot shortly after the Queen had ceremonially pressed a button in Aberdeen which activated the pipeline by which oil was brought ashore from the Brent Field in the North Sea. Our scene was to be a spoof on that event and so I turned up on a clifftop near Brighton in a beautiful yellow suit and hat. I walked to a platform mike to act out our version of the ceremony and give the little speech that had been written for me – but the director hadn't told me what was to happen next. I suppose he wanted me to be as surprised as the viewers.

I pressed the button and simultaneously they aimed a pressurised jet of water from a fire hose right at me. It was a miracle the force of it didn't take me over the cliff edge. As it was it hit me full in the eyes and knocked me flat on my back.

I heard hoots of laughter all around me and some of the production assistants came running over to me but I could not get up. It felt as if my eyes had been knocked back into my head.

'Was it a take?' I mumbled, with commendable altruism.

'Yes,' someone reassured me.

A couple of people supported me back to my hotel where they let me lie down while a make-up girl bathed my eyes. I could hear a man's voice saying, 'Come on, Jeannette, buck up. We've got work to do.' Then he spoke again, to one of the girls. 'You've got to get her ready because we're ready for the next shot. For goodness' sake, get her on her feet. We've got a schedule to keep to.'

My eyes were red and painfully swollen but the crew got me back into place at the cliff top where, to my amazement, I found they wanted me to do the same shot again. I felt like going home, but they promised that this time they would film a bit further away from the cliff, and aim the water lower. It was a marvellous scene but, by golly, it hurt! Still, it was a pleasure working with that crazy Rutles gang who do things like this all the time. The miracle is that they all survive intact.

By an odd coincidence my husband, Ken, as Drilling Manager for British Petroleum, who owned the Brent Field, would have been at the real inauguration ceremony if he had not resigned from the company only a short time before.

In another Rutles show I had to perform a tree-planting ceremony after negotiating a path through a field full of prostrate drunks. I delicately picked my way over them, threw the traditional spadeful of earth on to the sapling – and it wilted and died before my eyes. In a later sequence, I strode up to a house, banged on the door, and the whole building collapsed. The zaniest sketch of all had more than a touch of Candid Camera to it. I was sent to stand in a genuine cinema queue, dressed as the Queen and carrying a concealed microphone. People in the queue started muttering, 'What's she doing here?' I felt a fool. Nobody talked directly to me, but I could hear a lot of whispering going on. I got to the front of the queue, at which point an actress was substituted for the real cashier.

As the Queen, I of course had no money. I said, 'I want to see the film, but I've got no money.'

The cashier replied firmly, 'Who do you think you are? If you've got no money, you can't go in.'

I fumbled in my bag, saying, 'But I haven't got any. I don't carry money.'

'In that case, you can't come in,' the girl said.

Hardly brilliant dialogue but it was not scripted; we had just been told to ad lib. I could hear people in the queue whispering, 'Isn't she that woman we've seen on the telly?' 'It can't be the Queen. It must be the woman who looks like her.'

I stepped back from the queue and started fumbling in my bag again, then I walked up to the commissionaire, another 'plant', who was standing by the doors which led into the auditorium. I asked in my plummiest voice, 'May I please come in?'

'Have you got a ticket?' he said gruffly.

'No. You see, I've just come from Buckingham Palace but I'm sure my son will pay.'

'You can't come in here without a ticket. Who do you think you are – the Queen?'

'But I must go in!'

'Not without a ticket.'

'I'm going to phone Philip,' I said, very firmly, and went over to a phone box in the lobby where I pretended to make a call. After a while I went back to the commissionaire who said resolutely: 'It ain't no good, missus, I'm not letting you in.'

The cameras had been placed some distance off for this sequence, and the people in the queue, who really wanted to go to the cinema, could not see them. They were visibly wondering what on earth was going on, which was just what the director wanted.

A spoof just as funny was set up for The Dave Allen Show. He and I were both dressed in military outfits and set astride two fine horses in the grounds of a stately home. I dismounted to take the salute at a dais, and he came over to stand by me. As the march past, meant to represent the Trooping of the Colour, began, something exploded and covered us in black smoke. All planned, of course. Then, in the next sequence, still covered in black soot, I waved to a courtier who brought a huge pike over to me. I took the weapon from him and chased Dave Allen towards some woods.

I was just wondering how far I should chase him when I saw some Red Indians come leaping and whooping towards me. I couldn't stop in case the cameraman was still shooting so I ran straight into this ferocious but puzzled-looking band. It turned out that Benny Hill was filming on the other side of the same location, and these Indians were in one of his chase sequences. I wonder if our cameraman got a shot of me running with that heavy pike held aloft right into a band of Red Indians? If he did, it would be a classic worthy of 'It'll Be All Right on the Night'.

I made quite a mark opening the Jim Davidson Show on a number of occasions. The first time I was being driven along in a Rolls-Royce. In fact, Jim Davidson was with me in the car, lying on the floor in the back, though he could not be seen from outside. The Rolls stopped in Shepherd's Bush High Street where I stepped out to look into the window of a TV and hi-fi shop. A television in the window was showing the beginning of the Jim Davidson Show, with Jim walking along a street in the East End of London. A man looking in the window with me magically produces a chair, and I sat down to watch the start of the show. It was a wonderfully effective introduction to the show.

For another sequence I sat in a huge bed, complete with sceptre and orb, and had to push people out of the way to get a better view of my television set. Then there was the time I was sitting watching the Jim Davidson Show surrounded by corgis, with a TV dinner on my lap. The corgis, naturally, ate the dinner.

When I joined The Grumbleweeds for their zany television show, some of the other guests – Bernard Manning, Frank Carson, Faith Brown, and Alvin Stardust – were talking about what the Queen would or would not do. One of them said, 'I bet the Queen wouldn't take a beer. How about you?'

'Why don't you offer me one?' I said, and was handed a huge stein of beer. It looked so funny that everybody just folded up. A photographer on the set took what he thought was one of the photographs of the year – it looked as if the Queen was sipping from a huge glass of beer, which is something she would never do, or would she?

On the show itself, a group of us were filmed drinking beer when a really scruffy young girl walked on to the bar set. She looked at all of us then turned to the camera and said, 'Gee! I thought you told us there were going to be some famous people here.' None of us knew this line was to be delivered, and we all cracked up.

Later The Grumbleweeds sat me down for an interview but every time I opened my mouth to talk they spoke over me. None of it was scripted, and it was so funny that by the end I had tears running down my cheeks. On another show of theirs, I managed to get a few of my own words in when I read out a set of 'football results'.

In more serious vein, I was slipped into the audience for a live David Frost show a few days after the anti-royal M.P., Willie Hamilton, had made some particularly disparaging remarks. He called the Queen Mother an old age pensioner, attacked Princess Margaret because he said she didn't work for her keep, and said the Queen was a 'faded person'. He also said some very unpleasant things about Princess Anne, claiming the photographers had to work very hard to make a plain girl pretty on her wedding day.

David Frost asked me how I felt about all this. I said that if I were Princess Anne's mother, I'd have felt very upset about what had been written about her. 'I think that's what the public in general and Fleet Street in particular forget,' I said. 'The Queen is not just our monarch.

She is also a mother, and has feelings for her daughter. When she reads stories talking about her daughter as if she's an ugly duckling, it must hurt her. She is a woman who thinks very dearly of her daughter, and not enough consideration is given to her personal feelings.' I think it's a great shame that the Queen has to endure a lot of this sort of carping but is prevented by protocol from hitting back.

I seem to have been to most of the televised studios around the country, and appeared on most of our popular series. For a sketch with The Two Ronnies, they did a dance outside a building which was a lookalike of the Tower of London while I came to its door in my royal robes, put a milk bottle out, and gave the two of them a real old-fashioned look.

I went to Holkham in Norfolk to take part in a James Burke show about dreaming. The presenter was explaining how dreams occur, and the reasons for them. I was called on to act in a dream sequence where I would walk out on to the most beautiful sandy beach I have ever seen, say a few words to James Burke then pin a medal on his chest. As I was pinning the medal on, my heels sank into the sand. We needed quite a few takes to get it right.

Another beach scene, though it was a studio mock-up this time, featured in an appearance I made with Gloria Hunniford in Belfast on her 'Good Afternoon, Ulster' programme. Gloria was dressed up in a bathing costume as if she was on a beach, and I was driven, dressed as the Queen, into the studios in a Rolls-Royce. I walked around shaking hands, as if I were inspecting the studios.

Another time I stood at the rail of a motor boat to be delivered, very seasick, to an edition of The Mersey Pirates Show in Liverpool. The nicest thing about this appearance was the rousing cheer I got from a crowd of children who had been told only that a 'very important person' would be coming to visit them.

I managed to keep a straight face while three comedians did their best to shatter my composure in a show hosted by Bernie Winters, 'Make Me Laugh'. I met up with the lovely Bernie again when my daughter, Carol, went on his show 'Who's Baby?' Jim Davidson, Gareth Edwards and Frank Bruno were also there with their mothers, and Dana was there with her daughter. The panel could not guess who was Carol's mum.

I was put into a straight documentary show as 'the Queen', evaluating the work of two newcomers who had produced some amazing puppets of well-known people, including the royals. In my Queen character, I asked them if they had ever photographed the royal family and they replied with a terrific picture of their puppet caricatures of the Queen and Prince Philip. I still have that photograph on a wall in my home, and we know how well Roger Law and Peter Fluck went on to do with their 'Spitting Image' series.

For some reason, North Wales is not the location I would automatically associate with a royal rib-tickling venue but that was where I went to take part in a television comedy show. In one sketch I came out of the Deganway Castle Hotel to find a taxi waiting for me and a tramp standing nearby, watching. I am about to get into the taxi when the driver asks to see my money. I stand back in amazement.

'I am the Queen of England, how dare you ask me for money?' I say. He replies in Welsh, 'I don't have anyone in my taxi unless they can afford it.'

I stand there, very unhappy and miserable, and the tramp comes up to give me a little purse. When I open it up, there are coins inside with the Queen's head on them. The tramp holds one up to the driver, pointing to the head on the coin and then to my face and I am allowed into the taxi, after all.

In another sequence, I come out of the hotel calling for a taxi. A motorbike pulls up, a uniformed chauffeur riding it. I jump on to the back of the motorbike and am driven into the distance.

I made an appearance at Wembley Stadium for the Cilla Black show 'Surprise, Surprise'. A housewife who had always wanted to be a footballer ever since she was a young girl dreamed of being presented with the F.A. Cup and put in a coach to drive round the stadium to the cheers of the crowd. Cilla arranged for her to dribble a football on the Wembley turf with the West Ham player Trevor Brooking, then to mount the steps at the centre of the main stand where I presented her with the cup. Afterwards she was driven round the stadium in a coach while a recording of a cheering crowd was played. The girl was over the moon, and I got such a kick out of helping to fulfil her dream.

Soccer was also the theme when I was fielded in the team of 'The Six O'Clock Show' at a sports ground where Danny Baker kicked a ball at goal. The camera followed the ball – and there I was, dressed in the regalia, to catch it in the goalmouth.

My television appearances went international as film crews started turning up from all parts of the world. 'Good Morning, America' featured an interview with me, and Paul Hogan, the Australian comedian who has made such an impact with his lager advertisements, contacted me when he was filming in England. He used me in a 'Paul Hogan Show' sketch set on the beach at Brighton. He and some of his compatriots marched past along the beach, wearing knotted handkerchiefs on their heads, and solemnly saluted me. I took the salute royal-style but once again found my shoe heels slowly sinking into the sand. High heels and beaches clearly don't suit but the director liked the effect so much they left it in.

I even appeared on a Los Angeles radio show, beamed from the Kensington Palace Hotel. The joint compères of the show, Ken Minyard and Bob Arthur, brought a couple of hundred of their listeners over on a holiday to Europe which was to include attendance at the recording of a 'Ken and Bob' show. The American compères said they had heard a lot about me, and arranged for me to be brought into the hotel ballroom then conducted to a seat on the stage. There, Bob and Ken interviewed me as if I were really the Queen. 'How are you, Your Majesty? How does one like to meet the people from America?'

I had no prepared lines, and ad-libbed some queenly responses. 'Yes, I do love to meet my colonists over here,' I said. The audience pitched in with their questions, still talking to me as if I were really the Queen. To this day, I don't know if they had been told the truth.

My big screen career began when I was selected as the 'well-dressed lady' needed to appear in 'Custer's Thirteen', an American film about a wealthy young man who has to marry very quickly in order to secure an inheritance. I was one of the thirteen possible wives he considers. I had to walk in to the room, shake hands, answer a few questions, walk around a bit, then walk out. I enjoyed being on my 'own' film set for the first time, but I have to report I did not win Mr Custer.

I was a cocktail party guest in another American film, 'Tomorrow Never Comes', in a scene filmed at a beautiful country house at Chesham.

When the American comedian Chevvy Chase made a film called 'The European Tour' at Twickenham Film Studios, I was back in my lookalike rôle, along with lookalikes of Prince Charles and Princess Diana.

Our home-grown comedian, Eric Sykes, also conscripted me for a part in his re-make of 'The Plank', a silent film classic in which a man walks all over London with a plank.

When I turned up at the shooting location, a girl walked up to me and said 'I'll take your luggage for you', and picked up a huge suitcase containing my 'royal' equipment.

'No, please, it's very heavy,' I said, but she insisted. And that was my introduction to Joanna Lumley who was wonderful to me throughout the making of the film.

As I mixed on intimate terms with film people I thought back to my childhood visits to the cinema, and how I'd dreamed of being an actress. I had achieved that ambition in a totally unexpected way, all due to my very good fortune – the accident of birth which gave me a likeness to the Queen.

CHAPTER FIVE

1977 and All That

It was the year of the Queen's Jubilee, 1977, when the nation would celebrate her twenty-five years on the throne. It was going to be a long, hard year for her – and for me, too. In her Jubilee year, many people wanted the Queen to grace their events but, when she could not accept their invitation, were more than happy to take me as the next best thing.

I began my appearances that year with a trip over to Belfast to guest on Gloria Hunniford's show 'A Taste of Honey'. Northern Ireland was a place I was wary of going to; I had refused to make personal appearances there in the past because of the security risks. However, a radio link with Gloria a few days before had been so successful, and she was such a sweet, charming lady, that I decided to go.

She took me off to Stormont Castle, which was the seat of the devolved parliament until the troubles of the early 1970s. We could not go in because it is locked up and deserted now, but we did have a look around. Then we went to a big store in Belfast where Gloria was filmed stopping people to ask them, 'The Queen doesn't come to Belfast – how would you greet her if she did?' People were so courteous to me. Most guessed, of course, that I was not really the Queen but the doubtful expressions of people who spotted me and were not absolutely sure made good television.

I thought that with the political situation there, people would be averse to royalty but nothing could have been further from the truth. People would grasp my hand and say 'It's nice to see you', and I'd know they really meant it. When I asked them about attitudes over there, they would say, 'Well, we're as British as you are, dear.' They seemed to want to make a real point of their Britishness.

Just a few days later I was off a bit further afield, to St John's, the capital of Canada's province of Newfoundland, for the first broadcast of a Canadian Broadcasting System television show, 'Ninety Minutes Live'. I flew over on the same plane as two Monty Python veterans, Michael Palin and Graham Chapman, who were also booked to do the show so I knew from the start it was going to be very lively.

I was told to change into my queenly regalia at the hotel, and a Rolls-Royce was sent to collect me and drive me to the studios. This sequence was put 'in the can' and shown to the audience at the tiny but ultra-modern studios, and to the viewing audience, as the show was networked. Meanwhile I was waiting in the Rolls, hidden away in the parking lot, and at the appropriate moment was driven right into the studio where I was greeted by the show's interviewer, who said, 'This is a great year for you, isn't it, Your Majesty? It's lovely to see you back in Canada again, and we're very grateful that you've decided to grace our studios on the occasion of our first performance of this show . . .'

He went on and on. When he had finished his flowery welcome, I said how delighted I was to be there, and that unfortunately my husband could not make it. I said one or two things about the family, all of which had been scripted and rehearsed, then I got back into the car and was driven off round the back of the studios. I went into a changing room, got out of the regalia and put on a cocktail dress. I then made another entrance this time treated as Jeannette Charles, one of the line up of guest artists on the show. The two Monty Python fellows were there, along with a New York broadcaster called Bretty Murphy, and an outrageous American called Uncle Nugent.

That show was so funny that I was in tears by the end. The Monty Python pair kept butting in and taking over, no matter who was being interviewed. It might have looked a bit pushy and rude but the audience and I loved it. Their ad-lib dialogue was like machine-gun fire, fast and deadly. I saw the video of the show afterwards, and the camera kept panning to me. I was in hysterics, just crying and crying with laughter.

Back home, I was taken down to Fleet Street for a walk-on role in a short political comedy called 'Marcia'. Harold Wilson was still Prime Minister, and a lot of political gossip centred on Marcia Falkender, a member of his Downing Street staff. I changed into a beautiful outfit and strolled along Fleet Street while Peter Jones, John Junkin and Jon Pertwee, walking in the other direction, shouted 'Hello, Liz', and stopped to have a chat with me. The film was released as a B feature and was very funny, with a red-haired Barbara Castle lookalike and a lot of very clever fun poked at the Labour Party.

A Bavarian television channel came over to London to complete a film about a little boy who desperately wanted to see the Queen of England. It was a six-part series, and in the earlier parts the boy has searched and searched all over England without success. In this the final part he looks all over London unsuccessfully, finally giving up his quest. He gets into a taxi to take him to London Airport when he spots the

Queen (guess who it really was!) sitting at a table in the Hard Rock Café in Piccadilly, only a sceptre's throw away from Buckingham Palace, surrounded by children. It was the sort of child's-eye fantasy which the continentals seem to love.

The boy was brought into the café for the final scene of the film where he sat down and spoke to me. And, of course, a crowd gathered round us. Tourists wondered what was going on, and whether the Queen was really sitting in the café. Drivers saw a crowd gathering on the pavement and stopped to see what was going on. We caused a traffic jam on central London's busiest street, which brought the police along, too.

'Oh, it's you!' was all they said.

I was interviewed during this royal year by Barbara Howarth, a famous CBS interviewer, who was sent over especially from New York. She came to my house and interviewed me walking round the garden, asking me about the way I lived as Jeannette Charles with my family. Then we went into London and, at my suggestion, they filmed me walking all the way along Regent Street. I said that if we started early, we could get in quite a bit of walking up and down, and collect the reactions of passers-by on the way.

So we started off down Regent Street. Barbara carried a hand microphone, and I was wired for sound with a clip-on microphone. As we walked, she was asking me about how I felt about the royal family as I was growing up, and about my sister and myself, who are approximately the ages of Princess Margaret and the Queen. She asked me what I remembered about them as young Princesses, and I told her how my mother used to buy the knitting patterns of the woollen garments the Princesses wore, and copy them for us. I suppose it was the austere equivalent of today's copying of Princess Diana's elegant clothes.

I talked about my delight in royalty ever since I was young, how they are a much loved part of the fabric of society in this country. I talked about my childhood memories and was getting quite animated when I looked around to find Barbara gone!

I switched off my microphone and whirled round to the cameraman. 'I don't understand,' I said. 'Where's Miss Howarth?'

'Oh, don't worry, she'll be back.'

'But where's she gone?'

He shrugged. 'I don't know, she just ran.'

So we waited, and waited. And sure enough, as we waited, people passing by started slowing down, glancing sidelong, stopping and staring. Some even came up to me and asked me for my autograph. A couple of coaches went past, and the passengers were hanging out of the windows, taking photographs and waving.

I'd been on television quite a lot over the past two or three years, and I assumed they were acknowledging me as Jeannette Charles and not as the Queen. Whichever, the crowds were building up, drivers were hanging out of their car windows, and the cameraman had started filming again, getting some great shots of all this.

'So this is why Barbara's disappeared,' I thought. 'To get this sort of film for the show.' Then, as quickly as she'd vanished, there she was again, carrying a couple of parcels.

'I'm terrible sorry, I just had to do some shopping,' she said. We started walking down the road together when, once more, she ran off, this time into Hamley's.

I said to the cameraman, 'What now?'

'Well, I guess she doesn't have much time for shopping. Later on this evening, after we've seen the rushes and we feel everything is okay, she'll be on her way back to America because they want this as quickly as possible.'

Barbara came back again, but every once in a while on that walk down Regent Street she would pop off into an alluring shop. And so it went on. Our half-hour walk was turning into a two-hour marathon.

I was getting pretty hungry and tired and suggested to the film crew that I should call in at a hamburger joint to get something to eat. One of the technicians obligingly played waiter and went to a café to get some sandwiches and coffee which he brought out to us. There we were, standing on the corner of Regent Street, eating our sandwiches and drinking our coffee. More great shots for the cameraman, I suppose, but it's a morning I look back on with a great deal of bewilderment. At first I thought Barbara had been just plain rude to walk off and leave me, but I later came to the conclusion she had done it to produce the effect of me on my own surrounded by crowds of shoppers. It was very effective.

When we had finally finished with Regent Street, we went over to the Hyde Park Hotel where I changed from my two-piece and hat into a very pretty pink dress, teamed with pearls and a paste brooch. They had rented a very grand room there for an inside interview, and I remember the cameraman looked through the lens and said, 'This is just like the cover of a chocolate box. If we didn't know who you were, I would assume you were the Queen.'

I'm glad to report that I heard later that the film and interview were a great success on American television. I was slotted in between Lena Horne and Liza Minnelli, which says it all.

A crew also came over from the American 'Laugh-In' television show and turned the front room of my house into an *ad hoc* studio. They made a little frame I could sit behind to deliver my lines. For example, a voice off screen might ask, 'Where's your hubby?' and I'd call out, 'Philip, are you ready?' Then another voice would say, 'I'll be ten minutes.' They recorded thirty-two such sequences, and this exposure went a long way towards getting me known in America.

I was called over to New York to appear in a fabulous satirical variety show they have there called 'Saturday Night Live'. It's one of the longest running shows ever, and every American knows of it. The show's format is always based around a VIP guest, and on this particular week the guest was to be the Queen of England – or, rather, the closest they could get to her.

I turned up at the NBC studios in Rockefeller Center, and we started the rehearsal, with the whole of the show's cast, John Belushi, Dan Aykroyd, Eric Idle, Jane Newman and Gilda Radnor, seated around a big table. The script ordained 'Jeannette Charles as Queen starts a Frank Sinatra song'. So I started singing and, my God, it was awful. Everybody fell about laughing until one of them said, 'Okay, Jeannette, I think we can do without that, thank you,' and scratched my song from the script. My singing voice had not improved since my stint at the Intimate Theatre.

We were ready for the show which was to be a big milestone in my career. I went back to my dressing-room, which was more like a hotel suite, to change and make-up. There was a knock at the door and in walked a little man who said, 'I'm from AFTRA, the American Federation of Theatre and Radio Artists, and I've come for your union fees.' 'I beg your pardon,' I replied, 'but I don't belong to your union. I'm an Equity member in England.' 'That's not good enough over here, lady. You got to join our union and give us two-thirds of your fee for tonight.'

'I'm not going to do it,' I said angrily. 'I think it's highway robbery.'

He shrugged and said, 'Well, put it this way: if you refuse to sign, we'll black the show. We'll inform the other unions, and they'll join with us, particularly the electricians. They'll pull out the plugs and the studio will be in darkness. It's that simple.'

I was nearly in tears. I'd been so looking forward to my momentous night and now this had happened. I didn't understand it at all, and thought the union representative had been trying to frighten me into doing something that wasn't necessary. I called one of the studio staff in and told him everything, and he said, 'Yes, he's telling the truth. We're very sorry, Jeannette, but you have to join. You can't go on unless you do join this union.'

I asked why I hadn't been warned and had all this union business organised beforehand. Apparently it can never be organised in advance because an artist has to be actually doing the performance before the union can ask for their fees. Furious, I arranged for two-thirds of my fee to be deducted and given to the union, and the other third to be sent to my agent in London – which meant that after paying my agent's commission and tax I would be working for nothing.

I was most upset to run into union trouble again. I thought I had left all that behind in London. However, it has stood me in good stead on my subsequent visits to America. If I'm asked if I'm member of AFTRA, I can say, 'Yes, I am.' I'm a provisional member, which means I don't have to pay yearly fees, only a quarterly fee to cover the period in which I am performing.

I shrugged off this setback and went over to the studio where Eric Idle opened the show with a monologue. He said that for many years Americans had been having a wonderful time using English words without permission, and had never paid for them. Well, now was the time of reckoning. As England was now in dire financial straits, he would charge them for every English word they used. Americans love anything English, and the studio audience roared with laughter at the sketch.

Then he said, 'We have a very special guest here tonight, ladies and gentlemen. Please give a big hand . . .'

And down the steps I came, dressed in a flowing gown. It was a very big moment for me. I had been on chat shows and comedy programmes before but here I was facing a mammoth, coast-to-coast television audience, live. Walking downstairs in a long gown is not easy at the best of times but I managed it safely, keeping my head up, shook hands with Eric and sat down.

Eric reiterated, 'Because England is going through such a very bad time, the English need to raise money. By the way, that's why I'm hosting the show, because we need the money. And that's why the Queen is here.'

Another artist on the show was dressed up as a Canadian Mountie. He came on to the stage as Eric explained how the Queen would help raise money. 'Every time the Mountie groans, more money will be sent in.' At which point I walked up to the Mountie, raised my gown a little and pretended to knee him in the groin. He collapsed with a moan, and I walked demurely back to my seat. The audience roared. Eric picked up a collection box, which had a few coins in it, and went around the audience jangling it, pretending to collect money.

He thanked me for my efforts, then announced another sketch he had dreamed up for the show. 'The Queen has graciously consented to be auctioned off to the highest bidder, to raise money for her country.' He sat me by a huge clock on which sums of money were painted instead of hours. In the background were a row of people sitting by mock telephones. The auction was to be staged as a spoof telethon.

I settled down in my seat, took out a pair of knitting needles with some knitting already attached to them, and pretended to knit. The phones started ringing, and the first bids came in. 'Five dollars,' 'Ten dollars,' 'Twenty dollars,' called out the switchboard operators.

The lights then went up in a different part of the studio and another sketch was performed. Every once in a while, the focus of attention would be brought back to me, the clock and the telethon. Then the cameras would turn to another sketch, and come back to us later. I'd hear the telethon team saying things like, 'Credit cards? Yes sir, we can accept that.' Between these shots, a longer piece of knitting was handed to me. The show went on for an hour and a half, so by the end my knitting stretched for yards across the studio floor. It looked ridiculous, and very funny.

Later I went to Los Angeles to appear in 'The Red Foxx Show' at the ABC studios. Red was the black vaudeville performer who was cast in the American version of our 'Steptoe and Son', which was known out there as 'Sanford and Son.' For years it was the highest rated show in America, then Red decided he wanted to have his own variety show. A pilot show was set up and I was recruited, along with a President Carter lookalike, to launch it with Red. As a publicity build-up, the President Carter lookalike, Walt Hanna, and I were driven in an open Rolls-Royce limousine along Sunset Boulevard, through Los Angeles, and up to the gates of ABC in a tickertape welcome.

Walt Hanna and I ran through our sketch, in which we were to be filmed walking along the studio corridors. We set off, and as we walked we exchanged reminiscences about our respective lookalike careers. We became so engrossed in the conversation that neither of us heard the crew member shouting directions to us. Instead of making a right turn along another corridor, we kept straight on, and ended up walking right out of the studio building. Someone had to come and get us and put us in the right direction.

The ABC studios are vast, and I had my own dressing-room which seemed to be miles away from where the filming was taking place. I took a lunch break, and when it was time to go back for shooting I had no idea where I was. I didn't know if I was on the first floor, the third floor, or where. I decided my best option was to get into a lift and try each floor. I must find my way then.

As I stepped into the lift, I saw a man who looked very thin and pale with almost white hair. I, of course, recognised Dick Van Dyke because I'd been a regular viewer of his show. He'd spent a lot of time in a sanatorium, which explained his drawn appearance but he had a lovely twinkle in his eye still, and said to me, 'Well, your face looks familiar.'

'I'm working on "The Red Foxx Show" as the Queen.'

'Ah, I *knew* your face was familiar.' He stood back and executed a deep theatrical bow then said, 'I could do with you in my show.'

The man with him said, 'If we could fit you in, would you like to have a part in Dick's show, honey?'

I said I would, but, more important at the moment, could they tell me which floor I should get out on?

Dick's companion explained we were heading for the third floor whereas I needed the first. I should wait and take the lift down shortly. We reached the third floor, and who should step into the lift but Mary

Tyler Moore, Dick's partner in his show for all those years.

They had a chat then Dick said, 'We've got a very special person here, Mary. Be nice to her.' So I travelled down with Mary, and got out at the first floor. Unfortunately, it was the wrong one because the studio I was looking for was on a sort of mezanine floor. I finally managed to film my sequence with Red, which involved him walking in and me introducing him to the audience, at which point he said 'Gee, Elizabeth', jumped into my arms, and we both fell in a heap on the floor. That was the opening of the show.

A couple of days before the actual Jubilee Year anniversary day, I went early in the morning to the Victoria Statue in front of Buckingham Palace for a splendidly staged picture which Kent Gavin, the *Daily Mirror's* award-winning photographer, had planned. He was a regular royal photographer, and had often thought how exhausted the Queen must feel after all the walkabouts she was doing that year. To illustrate this, he wanted me to sit on the pavement across from Buckingham Palace, rubbing my tired feet.

A taxi collected me from my home and took me to the Victoria Statue for six o'clock because we had to get the photograph taken before crowds of tourists turned up to smother it. I was dressed in a beautiful gown, and carried a small crown with me. I got there a bit before Kent, who came running up to me, loaded with cameras. I sat down on the pavement with the crown in place but took my shoes off.

I don't know what they were doing out at that time of the morning but we kept drawing little clusters of tourists, most of them Americans. That sort of backdrop would have spoiled the picture, of course, so I had to keep getting back into the taxi to be driven round the block while we waited for the crowd to break up.

At one time, when Kent was about to take another shot, a car stopped and an American got out to run over and bow to me as I sat on the pavement, nursing my feet.

'Your Majesty, is it all right if I take a photograph as a souvenir for my family back home?'

I mumbled something and I could see that Kent just wanted the man to disappear. He took his photograph, and I've often wondered about that family in America who have a snapshot of me which they must show to their friends to prove that when the Queen of England gets tired, she just sits down on the pavement, kicks off her shoes, and rubs her poor, tired feet.

Kent managed to get a fabulous picture, with Buckingham Palace in the background, which was carried in the centre spread of his newspaper.

In Birmingham I took part in a television show, filmed at a hotel, which was a gesture of thanks to the Queen for her years of service. Jimmy Saville was there, Lord Montague of Beaulieu, Shaw Taylor, Libby Morris and her husband, Murray Cash. Each made a little speech saying what they thought about the Queen, how well she had done, how much her reign had meant to them. I came on at the end to say 'Thank you' for all the accolades.

A similar thing was set up at the spectacular Martini Terrace on top of New Zealand House in the Haymarket for a Canadian Broadcasting Service television recording. Michael Caine was there, along with Nigel Dempster, Patrick McNee and Joanna Lumley of 'The Avengers'. They all spoke up loyally for the Queen.

Willie Hamilton, who has made a name for himself by his attacks on royalty, was also there. No prizes for guessing which side he was on.

The interviewer asked me how I felt about the Queen, and about the reception given to me when I acted the part. I said that I could never see us being without our royal family, that they did a great job, and were worth every penny they were paid. I also said that from what I had observed during my appearances, people were very loving and loyal towards the Queen. Then the interviewer asked me to 'knight' him, which I duly did. These programmes can be very stilted unless a bit of fun is introduced.

That sense of fun was ladled out when I made another 'Q' programme with Spike Milligan. The scene was set in a supermarket where Spike was the manager, standing by the checkout till and taking the customers' cash to hand it over to me. I was collecting it because the royal family was short of cash. If any of the customers refused to hand over money, he hit them, shouting, 'Give me the money! Give me the money!'

I saw another side of Spike that day. His perfectionist streak was well to the fore when he examined a hairpiece to be worn by the actor who was portraying Prince Philip. He went wild, shouting that the hairs –

and Prince Philip does not have too many of them – were in the wrong place. I know he is a friend of the royals but I'm surprised he has such an intimate knowledge of Prince Philip's hair.

For The Goodies I posed as the Queen in a rush to get to an appearance, looking for a lift on a road in Portsmouth. A giant three-wheeler bike came along with two of The Goodies aboard. They fitted me into the space between them and pedalled off with me.

I sat in the royal box at the Theatre Royal, Stratford, East London, waving and smiling to four young, long-haired men supposed to be The Beatles in the Rutles film 'All You Need Is Cash'. Then I went onstage to ad-lib a conversation with them.

I co-starred with three corgis in a filmed advertising promotion for the comedy version of 'The Hound of the Baskervilles' which Peter Cook and Dudley Moore made. In the promotional film, in queenly character, I try to use a bit of royal influence to get my corgis into films. I say that it is *my* special year, and I deserve some special treatment. They say they need a big dog, an Irish Wolfhound, for the film, but I say that if my corgis jumped up, they would be big enough.

There was a sombre note to another performance of mine in 'Rachel in Danger', an Armchair Theatre television production about a girl who uncovers a plot to assassinate the Queen at a garden party. I was the Queen, of course, and Rachel, a young schoolgirl, manages to get the murder bid stopped by bodyguards who jump the would-be assassin just as his gun is trained on me. The best part of that film for me was the lemon-coloured dress and coat outfit I wore. It was beautiful, and afterwards I bought it from the production company. I still have it.

Laughter was the order of the day during a personal appearance I made at the Savoy Hotel during a party held to honour a record company boss who was leaving London to return to America. An incredible cast of showbusiness people he knew turned up to say goodbye, including Bruce Forsyth, John Le Mesurier, George Melly, Kenny Everett, Eric Idle and George Harrison. One by one they went onstage to say their piece, and I stepped up at the end to say how very sorry my husband and I were to have missed the pleasure of visiting him at his headquarters. I gave him a present, and wished him the best of luck.

In the Jubilee year I was also photographed near Buckingham Palace

Me, aged 17, perched on a wall overlooking Florence during my tour of Italy, when the paparazzi followed me to get a close up view of 'Principessa Elisabetta'.

My 21st birthday photograph.

Me alongside the painting which led to my 'discovery' when it was submitted for a Royal Academy exhibition. (*Rex Features*).

Me dressed as Florrie Ford 'Queen of the Music Hall' appearing at the Intimate Theatre, Palmers Green, in my quest for an Equity card. *(Evening News)*

I've always made sure my family are looked after. Here I am serving a meal at home to (left to right) daughter Carol, husband Kenneth, and sons David and Peter.

One of my favourite publicity shots.

Let down flat for a film publicity shot.
(Scope Features)

After filming at a stately home, the 'butler' served me a cup of tea.

A woman's work . . . *(Marc Henri)*

Let's pretend . . .

A pensive moment in my garden. Where *did* I leave that Land-Rover?
(Weekend)

Christmas With The Grumbleweeds was great fun.
(Granada Television)

With Russell Harty.
(London Weekend Television)

Kent Gavin, the Daily Mirror's award-winning photographer, often thought the Queen must have felt exhausted after all the Jubilee Year walkabouts. That was how I ended up, seated on the pavement, with my shoes off, in front of Buckingham Palace.
(Daily Mirror/Syndication International)

and the American Embassy with Walt Hanna, the Jimmy Carter lookalike I met in Los Angeles. I was then offered a hefty salary for a long season at Blackpool, walking up and down the Golden Mile as a living souvenir. I turned that down because I didn't want to spend so much time away from my family.

I did, however, accept a very short-term engagement to dress up as the Queen on a carnival float which paraded through London for a charity event. I had a crown on, and waved to the thousands of people lining the route, hanging out of windows or standing on rooftops. It gave me a real understanding of how the Queen must feel when she is surrounded by her happy, cheering people. Our float also featured a lady dressed as Queen Victoria and a mock multi-tiered cake. Derek Nimmo came round judging the floats, and we won an award.

A highspot of my Jubilee Year was when I was asked to partner Paul Stone, a magician who was to appear at a convention of the British Ring of the Magic Circle to be held in Hastings. He had won an award the previous year, and wanted to repeat the achievement with a novelty presentation.

I learned my rôle in the illusion while walking up and down the promenade, and the next day I waited in the wings while Paul began his act. He said he had a very important person backstage, recruited just a few minutes before, who was going to assist him. They were expecting somebody from the audience to appear so when I walked out, dressed as the Queen, a tremendous cheer went up. We went through a script Paul had written, which was about magic, and then he asked me for my crown, which looked real but was a fake. I gave it to him, and he put it into a box which he then proceeded to hit with a hammer. When he opened it afterwards there was nothing there. He then put his hand under the table and produced a crown which was completely undamaged and identical to the one he had taken from me.

I pretended not to be impressed or amused but clapped my hands and two Beefeaters came onstage to grab him and carry him, screaming, off into the wings.

Paul won two awards at the convention, including one for ingenuity. A lot of people wrote to me to say they had never seen such an unusual act performed by a magician, and apparently people still talk about it.

As the Royal Jubilee Year of 1977 drew to a close, I reflected that it had been a tiring time for me, but that Her Majesty must have been twice as exhausted. However, it had also been exhilarating, and the amount of love I'd seen expressed for her showed me that our services were going to continue to be in demand for quite some time.

CHAPTER SIX

Appearances – and a Queenogram

I was sitting quietly at home one day, when I heard a rat-tat-tat on the front door. I answered it, to find myself confronted by two men with huge, very wide shoulders.

I whispered to Ken, 'Who are they? They look like the Mafia.'

Ken laughed, which mystified the two men, who turned out to be representatives of The Showman Fellowship of Great Britain, an organisation which represents our travelling fairground workers. They had read about me in a newspaper, and came to ask if I would appear at one of their functions.

Some weeks later, I swept, dressed in royal regalia, into a glittering evening they staged at the Savoy Hotel, and delivered a speech acknowledging the efforts of the previous year by members of the Fellowship.

This was the first of my ceremonial appearances, and addressing gatherings in this way has become a regular feature of my repertoire.

Whatever my audience may choose to believe, I am never introduced as the Queen. Usually the chairman, or whoever is organising the event, will announce a surprise or special guest and I will make a grand entrance, accompanied by appropriate music like 'Land of Hope and Glory'. Generally, I am requested to make a speech, and for that I gather bits of information about the members of the audience.

I make a point of never beginning my speech: 'My husband and I'. Instead it will begin something like, 'Ladies and gentlemen, please be seated. It gives me great pleasure to be here this evening on your special occasion.' Sometimes I am called on to make awards to retiring employees of a business, or perhaps to give awards for individual achievement. A ceremonial sword is usually kept close at hand for me to use when performing mock knighting ceremonies, which are great fun.

Big companies particularly like this sort of thing to perk up their conventions and conferences, as well as their parties. I was brought in to surprise an American Express gathering in a West End hotel, where I remarked that my family found the credit card useful because we never carry money. The ripple of laughter the remark produced was only polite, and I got the feeling that the businessmen present may really have believed that I was the Queen. Well, even if that was the case, I couldn't very well walk round the room shouting, 'I'm not.'

For the opening of a shoe store in Sloane Square, I was driven around Knightsbridge in a horse-drawn carriage. Later, when I was seated in the store, an elderly passer-by came in and was offered a drink.

'No thank you,' she said. 'I've just come in to see that wonderful lady.' She just stood by the door, gazing at me, with a lovely smile on her face.

I joined a company party together with a President Reagan lookalike, which took the form of a river boat trip along the Thames, out past the flood barrier and back. I gave an introductory speech at the outset of the voyage, and was called on to wind up the proceedings with a closing address. The boat was late getting back and, as I was about to read my speech, the lights failed so the captain produced a huge torch to shine on my notes. I wonder if this sort of thing has happened to the Queen? I was put off the boat with my lookalike companion at Greenwich, where a number of boats were disgorging their passengers. They started cheering and waving, and kept it up until we were out of sight.

A similar thing happened when I turned up Thames-side to greet the staff of a hotel organisation as they arrived for a river trip. A big crowd gathered to shout and cheer me on, and I felt very exposed and uncomfortable because my appearances 'in character' are normally made within a more private venue.

I received a more sedate welcome at Wren's Old Hotel in Windsor where I joined an upriver Thames journey with a company's sales staff. The photographer hired for the event had a special device attached to his camera which enabled him to produce polaroid prints on adhesive paper. Each guest had a photograph taken with me, and the prints were stuck to souvenir key rings.

Delegates at a conference party for computer software salesmen at the London Hilton arrived expecting a serious talk but were delighted to be addressed by the very funny Clive James. Then came a fanfare of trumpets and I made my entrance, dressed in the full queenly regalia. The room fell completely silent until Clive broke the ice by saying, 'Now, gentlemen, Her Majesty just wants an informal evening.'

I did not have a prepared speech but Clive slipped me a piece of paper. On it were some notes for a very witty speech and I much appreciated his generosity in preparing them for me.

Science professors from all over the world had completed a symposium at Knutsford, Cheshire, when I addressed them. There were many Chinese among the delegates and I was amazed to find that, though small myself, I seemed to tower above them. Afterwards, as I joined in the delegates' cocktail party, these tiny Chinese gentlemen displayed a marked *penchant* for pinching my bottom. The woman who had arranged my appearance told me, 'They're just letting you know that, if you fancy them, they're available.' Oh well, I suppose it's the thought that counts.

I cut the cake at a Lyceum party given for a thousand guests from showbusiness and Fleet Street by Tony Elliot, owner of *Time Out*, to celebrate the 10th birthday of his entertainment guide magazine. I presented flowers to Laurie Purden, Editor of *Woman's Journal*, during a birthday party for her which included a fashion show introduced by Nanette Newman. Laurie was called onstage, there was a trumpet fanfare, my signature tune 'Land of Hope and Glory' was played, and I walked in with a 'lady-in-waiting'.

At a Mars regional sales conference and Christmas party in Blackpool, I was guest of honour and made a speech praising the sales force and describing the new products they were to be selling soon. Then I went over to a large box covered in silver foil, pulled a string, and out popped a girl carrying piles of the company's new 'Wispa' bar. I enjoyed that event tremendously because I came home staggering under the weight of enough Mars and Wispas to last me for months.

The Birmingham Exhibition Centre was my 'stage' for an appearance on behalf of a company which sold cavity insulation equipment. I would go off for a walk around the hall and usually returned, like the Pied Piper, with a bunch of people following me, pleasing my client no end.

A photographers' convention at Bournemouth, entitled 'Shooting for Gold', were surprised when I arrived to hand out the accolades. I told the gathering, 'My family, of course, never hires photographers. We have two in the family and use them because they come free of charge.'

A Len Crawford car showroom in Liverpool was the venue for a launch party for the Mini Metro. It was beautifully staged with a cavalcade led by a pipe band, and me in a Rolls-Royce with an 'ERII' numberplate. I stepped out, dressed in my regalia, to give a speech then went to a changing room to put on an afternoon dress for my walkabout.

When I was booked for a special event at a hotel's disco in Rhyl,

North Wales, a huge crowd turned up at the railway station to greet me. The hotel owner, a lively entrepreneur called Louis Parker, greeted me with a beautiful bunch of flowers. I was also presented with a live corgi, and someone laid a trick whoopsy on the pavement behind the dog. A photographer got a very funny picture of me standing there, holding the dog's lead, with the whoopsy plainly visible. They took the dog away from me afterwards. I'm glad I didn't have to keep it. I've never been a corgi person really.

A television reporter later interviewed me while we drove around in a car. At the end, he stepped out of the car, said 'Goodbye, Your Majesty', got on a bike and rode away.

The disco event was inspired by the fact that Prince Charles had recently been associated with a number of girls. A selection of young ladies was invited to parade in a beauty competition as prospective brides for the bachelor prince. I was heralded in as 'our very special guest' and sat in an ornate chair to interview the candidates and choose a 'bride' for Charles. They were lovely, sweet girls, but I don't think any of them looked like Diana.

It was back with the magicians again at The Room at the Top in Ilford, where I was the guest of honour when the British Ring of the Magic Circle installed Brian Miller as its president.

A very different assignment awaited me in Torquay, at an exhibition of heavy engineering equipment, when all kinds of giant tractors and earth diggers were lined up along the seafront. At the appointed time, the man who was employing me, Mr Turner of the Powell Duffryn Group, collected me from the Grand Hotel and drove me along the front in an open car. When we arrived at the spot where all the machinery was assembled, I walked around talking to people. I found myself talking to some of the competition, but Mr Turner didn't mind. He was so proud of his unusual guest, and I was a big attraction for the Powell Duffryn section. I enjoyed it greatly, but not as much as Mr Turner. It was great to see him having such a good time.

The General Electric Company staged a big surprise for their guests at a country hotel at Egham, Surrey, when they provided me with two corgis and had me stroll across the lawn overlooked by a giant conservatory where about eighty international guests were eating a buffet meal. Dozens of forkfuls of food halted in mid-air, and from the general hubbub one question rose loud and clear: 'What's *she* doing here?' I walked round the building to a side door and was escorted into the buffet. I was introduced, walked around talking to the guests, and found that a lot of them really believed Her Majesty had arrived.

Wilkins Tours is a company specialising in arranging British holidays for trans-Atlantic visitors, and they realised a long time ago that they could capitalise on the American fascination with our royalty. They have called on me many times to round off one of their tours by making a last-night appearance for their guests. On one occasion, they had a room at the Café Royal decked out to represent old cockney London, with beefeaters, a pearly king and queen, a town crier, a flower stall, and little flower girls. Towards the end of the evening, the town crier rang his bell and called out, 'Oyez! Oyez! Ladies and gentlemen, pray silence for Her Majesty.'

A fanfare of trumpets sounded and I walked into the room, regally dressed and very upright. The room fell totally silent and I felt, as I often do on these occasions, a strange sensation of power. I launched into my speech which thanked America for sending over all these tourists to spend their dollars with us, then I walked around the room, talking to everybody.

As I circulated, I could hear the excited whispers all around me: 'Oh, isn't it marvellous? Isn't it wonderful.' If people are really convinced by my act then I've done my job well, achieved the character to perfection. There's no reason to blow it.

More *mondain* American visitors will say things on these occasions like, 'I saw you on a television show in America'. But so many Americans get such a thrill out of thinking they've met up with our English royals that I don't give the game away unless I have to.

In another appearance for Wilkins Tours, this time at the Grosvenor House Hotel in Park Lane, the company's Managing Director was present and I was briefed to welcome him to London. I wished him the best of luck, and invited him to come over to Buckingham Palace for afternoon tea and cucumber sandwiches. After my speech, the tourists gathered around me and one of the couples asked me if they could see me again.

I said, 'I'm terribly sorry, but I'm rather busy at present and I don't live in London.'

Then I remembered that I would be in London the next day, shopping in Regent Street. They checked their itinerary and told me the time they would be out and about and, coincidentally, driving along Regent Street. At the appointed time the next day, there they were hanging out of the coach window, waving and blowing raspberries, while I waved to them from the pavement. God knows what people must have thought.

It was my turn to be staggered when I attended a celebration evening dubbed 'The World of Extravaganza' at the Holiday Inn in Plymouth. I found that the lobby had been transformed to take on the appearance of an airport. Two hundred and fifty guests had been flown in from all over the world, and in the lobby they were met by stewardesses and 'customs officers'. Each guest was given an individual passport and mock flight information was announced over the loudspeaker system, together with directions about duty-free shops. It was just like being at a real airport. Then the guests were taken into a mock-up of a Concorde aircraft complete with flight deck where a back-projected film and full sound effects gave the guests the impression they were aboard an aircraft which was touching down.

After the 'landing' they were escorted into the ballroom, which had decorated ballustrades, draped canopies, and moving cloud effects. As I entered there was a Royal Marine fanfare and a rendering of the National Anthem which brought all the guests to their feet. I rounded out the evening by knighting the Plymouth jeweller, Michael Spiers, 'Sir Mike' for his efforts in setting the evening up. He deserved it, too. He'd done an amazing job.

I was also at that Holiday Inn to give a royal send-off to the manager, or innkeeper as they are known in the chain, Peter Nannestad, who had completed three successful years there. I rounded off the evening by 'crowning' his successor, Thilo Thielmann.

Plymouth inhabitants may also remember me waving off a marathon from outside the offices of their magazine '*Spotlight*', and taking a march past of the town's scouts and girl guides.

I opened The Dome restaurant in the King's Road, Chelsea, where it was so packed they had to push people out of the way to make room for me at the microphone. I was looking out towards the main road, and with hundreds of faces pressed against the windows from outside it was like appearing in a goldfish bowl.

I was also invited to the opening of the boxer John Conteh's restaurant in the West End. Ken and I drove around *and* around looking for it, not particularly eager to go if the truth be told – I don't really like crowds on my nights off. But when I got inside I was lifted off the floor by two muscular men and carried through the crowd to the booth where John Conteh was sitting with 'The Greatest', Muhammed Ali. Both of them stood rigidly to attention to welcome me, and I had such a good time with them. They were both so friendly, and 'The Greatest' was just that.

Shortly after Prince Charles's son, Harry, was born, I went down to Ramsgate to open the first 'Prince Harry' pub in the country. (Actually the pub was about a hundred years old, and had been renamed.) In my speech I said how pleased I was to see that public houses were being named after my grandchildren.

The White Lion Pub at Putney fell into instant and unusual silence when I walked in one evening. I was taken to a seat where I gave a little speech about how much I liked to walk out amongst Londoners. I was just leaving when a lot of new customers turned up. They were so disappointed at missing the entertainment that I went back to my seat and the microphone and gave the whole speech again.

I get an incredible number of requests to turn up at birthdays, wedding receptions, anniversaries, and barmitzvahs. Peter de Savary, the man who put up the money for the British attempt to win the Americas Cup yacht race, visited Buckingham Palace a few days before his brother's marriage, and I suppose he got the idea there as to how he could add a little extra glamour to the wedding reception.

The couple, Nicholas and Jane, and their guests were in a marquee set in a huge garden when I walked in to give a speech, walk around, and be photographed with the family. A short while afterwards, I was also a surprise guest at a wedding held at a hall in Willesden Green. My method for this sort of assignment is to talk to whoever books me to find out what I can about the couple, where they met and that sort of thing, then weave the details into my speech.

A job which really touched me came about because Dave Clarke, the pop singer and drummer who had gone off to live in America, remembered a couple who lived next-door to his sister in Chingford. They had known him since he was a boy, going to school and playing in the street, and they were like second parents to him. I changed at the sister's home, then popped next door to walk into the couple's Ruby Wedding anniversary party. It was so beautiful. The old couple cried, and said it was an evening they would never forget. I thought it was tremendous that Dave had remembered them after all those years, and also gratifying that he had heard about me though he lived in Los Angeles.

Alex Bernstein, one of the owners of Granada Television, decided to surprise an old friend, an art dealer called Leslie Waddington, on his fiftieth birthday. The hardest thing for me was getting into the dealer's Belgravia flat unnoticed. I must have looked ridiculous with a scarf and dark glasses on, and a little case in my hand. But I managed to get into the flat without Leslie realising what was going on until I walked into the reception room 'in character'. The look of delighted surprise on his face made it all worthwhile.

Another birthday call was to Langan's, the famous London restaurant. I believed, for some reason, that the establishment was split up into small, private rooms, and expected to be shown into one of these. It was only when I got to the restaurant that I found I would have to walk across the vast, crowded front room to reach the table where my 'target' and his friends were having a celebration dinner. 'Land of Hope and Glory' was struck up and I stepped, dressed in the full regalia with tiara and jewellery, into a room which seemed to have hundreds of people in it. I couldn't back out, so I put my chin up and my chest out, and started out on the long walk.

As I strode through the room I heard the buzz of conversation stop, and chairs scraping as people stood up. By the time I reached my target table in the far corner, you could have heard a pin drop. I asked, 'Who is Ed Hinks?' and a bemused man said he was.

I delivered my speech to him, had a drink to toast his birthday, then 'knighted' him. Michael Douglas, Kirk's son, who is now an actor and producer, came over and stood near the table, looking absolutely perplexed. When I started to leave, everybody in the restaurant stood up to applaud and I walked out, smiling regally at customers to either side of me.

Richard Shepherd, the restaurant's co-owner, who oversees the kitchen, came out to say, 'I must have a photograph taken with you.' He told me later that there were a lot of Americans in the restaurant that night who had never heard of Jeannette Charles. He said it was the best spoof he had ever seen. It certainly gave Langan's a party spirit that night, and I was proud to have caused it. The *Daily Express* called my appearance a 'Queenogram,' and I'd say that's a pretty good description.

Even I was surprised when I got a call to go to the Sandhurst Military Academy to stand in for the Queen at a rehearsal for a Sovereign's Day Parade, held when the officer students graduate and receive their commission from the Queen. My daughter, Carol, drove me to the gates of Sandhurst, and we were directed to a ladies' cloakroom where I could hide until it was time to make my appearance. A Land-Rover was brought round and I climbed into the back of it, standing upright, while holding on to a bar while I was driven the half mile to the parade ground.

As we approached it, I could hear typical parade ground noises, orders being barked and soldiers marching. Several uniformed men working in the gardens that we passed stopped what they were doing and drew themselves crisply to attention when I came into view. I thought they would have known about the rehearsal, but perhaps they had not been told.

Then I saw the cadets drawn up in precision lines on the parade ground, and it was a beautiful sight. I dismounted to inspect them, and was escorted round by a burly Sergeant-Major with a twinkle in his eye. I walked around making small talk and shaking hands. It was all great fun, and what gave me a great fillip was the three rousing cheers the cadets raised for me at the end of my inspection. It was a wonderful spectacle and I loved the feeling of exhilaration it produced which I'm sure Her Majesty must have experienced, too, when she inspected the real parade.

An appointment of a more commercial nature awaited me when I went along to Caesar's Palace nightclub in Luton to open the show. I got myself ready in my robes and sat backstage, waiting for my call. Suddenly I heard applause and the unmistakable sound of a show in progress. Cilla Black, who was also appearing that night, walked by and spotted me.

'What are you doing here?' she asked.

'I'm here to start the show.'

'Well, it's already started,' she said, a surprised look on her face.

'I know,' I said. 'I can hear it.'

'They've obviously forgotten you. It just goes to show that the Queen's not always that important, doesn't it?'

I was paid my fee, but I went home very disappointed.

A more startling experience was when I was booked to address a big party in another nightclub. It turned out there were two hundred men in the club that night, every one of them dressed in the most beautiful women's clothes. They were all charming and polite, but when I make an appearance, I'm used to being the only queen.

Some of my voluntary appearances, made for love not money, have given me the greatest pleasure of my second career. One of the first such requests was to drop in on the eightieth birthday party of a lovely old lady called Lily who had set up a local drama circle and was still involved in charity work despite her age. When the organisers contacted me, I told them I would happily dispense with my usual fee. I turned up dressed to impress and Lily was thrilled. It was marvellous to see her surrounded by so many friends and relatives who clearly thought a lot of her. They put on a most impressive show of comedy sketches, singing and dancing.

I was called out on a similar mission to the birthday party of a sweet old lady who had reached the magical age of one hundred. I walked in wearing some of my most beautiful clothes and a tiara and, do you know, the dear old soul really thought it was the Queen arriving to deliver her telegram personally? She took it in good part when she was told afterwards by her relatives who I was.

When the Chelmsford District Council presented a 'Royal Variety Show' for pensioners in the town's Civic Theatre, I made a regal entrance in a beautifully embroidered gown with shoulder sash and a sparkling tiara. Escorting me were a mace bearer with a tricorn hat and another man with a ceremonial sword. It was a delightful piece of make-believe which gave so much pleasure to some lonely folk who were unlikely ever to see the Queen in person.

I have got so much out of opening local charity events, like the fête dubbed 'A Royal Summer Fair' by my village's Danbury School Association. It was advertised as, 'A majestic occasion for all the family.'

I prepare short speeches for these occasions, usually including something about the charity and the guests. And I may say something like, 'As there isn't a royal box, I'll come and sit amongst the audience.'

There was a royal box waiting for me at a charity show held in the Stratford, East London, Theatre Royal. I did, however, make one big mistake there. Gertrude Shilling, the lady who appears at Ascot in those enormous hats, was there. And, yes, she had a bonnet on about the size of a barrage balloon. During the interval, she visited me in the royal box and I said, 'It's rather lonely up here, why don't you stay with me for the second half?' She did, and I was hidden from the audience by her bonnet! I learned a lesson that night, and it's the only time I've been upstaged by a hat.

I presented awards for charitable work to volunteer workers at a Multiple Sclerosis centre in Didcot, Oxfordshire. I thought it tragic that people should be struck down by such a terrible disease, and was very impressed by the dedication of their relatives and the nursing staff. Another time, I attended a charity event for a group of handicapped people with Ronald Fraser, Clive Dunn, Jess Conrad and Bob Monkhouse. Bob's handicapped son was there in a wheelchair, and his devotion to the young man brought tears to my eyes.

I always chuckle when I think of the time I went to Brighton to make a speech and give out some awards for Amnesty International. They had taken over a section of the beach, and were serving hamburgers and sausages. I arrived in the evening as all this was going on, and they shone a lamp on me while I gave my speech. They were very receptive and appreciative, but when I got back to my hotel I was told that most of the audience were French and had not understood a word of my speech.

An Equity charity stages a football match each year, and I went to the Chelsea ground at Stamford Bridge for the game between a show-business team and a celebrity side. I performed quite well in the pre-match marathon hand-shaking session, but I didn't do so well when I had to kick off the ball to start the game. I missed it completely.

I also found myself invited onto a charity television spectacular in Los Angeles during one of my visits there. Bob Hope was starring, along with many familiar Hollywood faces, and I made a short speech. It felt great to be in such illustrious company, and to find so many people were prepared to make a charitable donation to be photographed with me.

But I do find I have to watch my step in some charity situations. There was the time when I attended a charity opening of a social club and was handed a speech just before I went on stage. When I started reading it, I found it poked fun at the royals so I abandoned the notes and made a speech off the cuff, which went down really well.

Another lesson was learned when I answered a request to sit in the royal box at a charity concert scheduled for the huge Free Trade Hall in Manchester. I turned up in mid-afternoon, hauling my very heavy suitcase, to find the place deserted. I banged and banged on a door until an old man answered to tell me, 'We don't let anybody in at this time of the day.' I explained why I was there, to appear in the show, and he said, 'Whoever is in charge of this hasn't advertised it properly. They just put a tiny poster on a pillar outside the hall – you can see it for yourself.'

I inspected this advertisement, which was just about visible, then asked the caretaker: 'Do you know how many tickets have been sold?'

'I'd imagine about fifty, if you're lucky.' He could see I was shocked to have come so far for such a poor house and sat me down and gave me a cup of tea. Then one of the other artists turned up, looking as worried as I felt. Finally, the young man who was responsible for arranging this disaster turned up. We gathered around him and asked, 'How many people are coming?'

'Oh, it's very sad,' he said. 'We didn't get to the radio in time.'

He had several other excuses, but the truth was he did not know how to stage a show of this kind. For example, he hadn't advertised, and the Free Trade Hall holds thousands. Marty Wilde had turned up, with his Wildcats group; there were dancers, singers, comedians, quite a cast. Nevertheless, the caretaker said there was no way he was going even to turn the theatre lights on for the few people who were likely to turn up. There happened to be a small theatre next-door to the Free Trade Hall so we all tramped over there. We found our dressing rooms and got ready for the event, if you'll excuse the expression. Our organiser didn't even know what a callsheet was, so we made one up for him, and staged the show ourselves.

Something under fifty people turned up, but I must say the cast staged a wonderful show. They put everything they had into it, as if they were appearing at the London Palladium. The tiny audience loved us.

When I was asked to attend a charity banquet for an organisation of which the Queen Mother was patron, the organiser was anxious that my presence should cause no offence so she telephoned Clarence House to clear it with them.

'Guess what?' she told me. 'An equerry said, "Mrs Charles is a delightful lady and we have never had cause to pass judgement on the way she conducts herself."' To me, it felt like a royal accolade.

CHAPTER SEVEN

Familiar Sights

Buckingham Palace is one of our national assets and has been of particular value to me. It is one of England's great tourist attractions, and is instantly recognisable to people all over the world which means I have been able to use a ready-made backdrop more illustrious than any theatre could offer.

It made the perfect eyecatching setting for a Crown Paint commercial I featured in. For this job, I was taken in a car to Westminster Bridge at six in the morning to meet up with someone called Jim who was to arrange the camera work. Westminster Bridge at that time in the morning is a pretty odd place to be, and my driver had a most uncomfortable time going up to any car which stopped near us to ask, 'Are you Jim?'

The other drivers would take a long look at him, then a curious one at me seated in the car behind. Their expressions were indescribable. One or two got a little indignant, and I could see my driver was not enjoying himself at all.

'Would you like me to do the asking?' I offered.

'Oh, no, madam, you just stay where you are.'

After he had approached about half a dozen cars with not a Jim in sight, a police car drew up by us. A policeman stepped out and walked to the side of our car. He looked inside, touched his hand to his helmet in an ironic salute and said, 'Good morning, madam. It seems that you have been creating something of a disturbance. What's going on?'

My driver explained who I was, and that we were waiting for Jim. The policeman had a good laugh, and just then the elusive Jim finally drove up. I got into Jim's car and he drove me to within a few yards of Buckingham Palace, where a film crew was waiting.

I was handed a heavy tin of paint and told to walk to the iron railings, turn to the right, then step forward and look as if I was examining the paintwork of one of the gates. I did this, and realised that a policeman inside the grounds was matching me step for step.

'Aren't you the lady I've seen on television?' he said.

'Yes, I am. but I can't stop and talk to you, because I'm working.' The director must be biting his nails. He didn't need a uniformed police constable in shot with me. But my new friend was not going to be put off.

'It's very nice to see you,' he said, and started chatting away. I tried to edge discreetly to one side of him and turned directly towards the Palace. I took a step forward then heard a voice shouting urgently: 'Run, Jeannette! Run!'

I turned, and a Rolls-Royce which had been parked nearby pulled into the pavement a few feet from me, and a back door was flung open. I ran as fast as I could to the car. I didn't know why I should, but I ran and jumped into the back. The front door was thrown open and a cameraman jumped in.

As we drove away, I looked out of the rear window and saw the reason for our sudden action stations. A small posse of policemen, presumably turning up for duty around the Palace, were heading towards us. We sped away and the lid of my tin of paint, which must have been loose all the time, came off. The paint poured out, cascading into the front of the car, all over the driver's feet. It lay in a pool on the floor, lapping around his heels. What a mess! The man, who also happened to be the producer of the film, a cheerful cockney character, said, 'Don't worry about it. I'll change the car tomorrow.' I still don't know if he meant it.

We drove away and I nodded off to sleep. I don't know where we went but when I woke up, we were at some kind of stately home which had a front gate just like the ones at Buckingham Palace. They paid a cheque to someone in an office for permission to use their gate in the rest of our filming. I got out and was provided once again with a tin of paint. I was given a brush, dipped it in the paint, and started painting the gates.

It seemed there were two people in charge, and they couldn't make up their minds about how much of the gates I should paint. 'Up to here, Jeannette,' said one. 'No, up to here,' said the other. By this time, we had attracted a bit of a crowd, and I could hear people whispering things like, 'That's the lady who looks like the Queen.'

The argument between the two bosses raged, and a woman came up to put her arm around me and say, 'There love, you go and stand over there. Don't you worry about a thing. I can see you're working very hard.'

She went over to the two production men and said, 'Make up your minds which of you is the gaffer. You're working the girl into the ground.' Then she backed off to stand with her husband and watch us at work. It was terribly funny but no one laughed. The two men finally made up their minds, and I finished painting the gate to their satisfaction. A professional painter was on hand to repaint the gates to their original condition and I was driven back to London in a Rolls-Royce still swimming with paint.

Jeannette Charles walkabouts arranged by magazines or television companies who wanted to photograph the reactions and double takes of passers-by soon became a regular feature of my life, and, of course, the favourite locations were around Buckingham Palace. When I was interviewed by an American television crew, we went along just before eleven o'clock in the morning to position ourselves at the Victoria Statue opposite the Palace in time for the arrival of the Guards when they march up from the barracks in Knightsbridge.

I was dressed very smartly in a yellow coat with matching hat, and stood amongst the crowd on the steps of the statue. There were a lot of people there, and I noticed an inquisitive American boy who had clearly spotted me. I heard him say to his father, 'Gee, is that really the Queen? Doesn't she look great?' He had two or three cameras slung round his neck and asked his father, 'Do you think I could take a picture of her?'

The father gave him a look which said without words, 'Now, you be respectful,' and seemed uncertain about what advice to offer his son. I pretended not to notice this was going on. I stood, looking straight ahead, until I heard a young voice say to me, 'Excuse me, Ma'am.' I looked down at the boy.

'Do you think I can take a photograph of you, and do you think I could have your autograph?' he asked.

I was very aware that the crew's camera was due to record me at this moment. 'I'm very sorry,' I said, 'but I'm taking the march past.' He looked so disappointed that as I had read somewhere that the Queen would be coming out on to the balcony, the next day I told him, 'Come along here tomorrow, and I'll give you a wave.'

The boy blushed scarlet but was obviously pleased. 'Thank you,' he said, and walked back to rejoin his father.

When the Guards had marched past and gone into the Palace, I told the crew I wanted to make sure I got away from the boy and his father who were still eyeing me so we went off very quickly to St James's Park where the crew also wanted to photograph me.

I realised I had to go to the lavatory. 'You really must excuse me,' I said to the crew. I went into the public lavatory in the park and heard a little girl's voice saying, 'I know it's the Queen. She just went into that toilet.'

A woman's voice, presumably that of her mother, said, 'That's ridiculous. Why would the Queen come out of the Palace and walk across the road to go into a public toilet?' The little girl started to protest, and the mother insisted, 'It's absolutely ridiculous. You're just being silly.'

The camera crew, meanwhile, had quietly lined themselves up to make sure they captured the expression on the faces of passers-by when I walked out of the lavatory. And, sure enough, as I walked out the mother's eyes nearly popped out of her head. She stepped forward to ask me hesitantly, 'Excuse me. I hope you don't mind me saying so, but you look so very much like the Queen. Er . . . are you?'

It was so funny that I really felt tempted to tell her I *was* the Queen, but I just couldn't bring myself to do it. 'Well, no. Actually I'm being filmed for American television,' I said indicating the camera.

I was asked for my autograph, which I gave, and the two of them went off very happy with their day's sightseeing. We continued around St James's Park, the cameraman got some great pictures of heads turning to look at me.

A Finnish magazine called *Hymy* pulled out all the stops to put together a photographic spread of me by various sights of London. The editor came over to arrange it, and we had a beautiful picnic together, complete with champagne, around the Victoria Statue opposite Buckingham Palace. They photographed me watching the Guards passing by and at Horse Guards Parade in Whitehall where the magnificent Life Guards sit astride their horses.

In those early days, I felt embarrassed just to walk in front of Buckingham Palace but the editor said wistfully, 'You know, Mrs Charles, the most wonderful picture of all would be for us to have you in the Palace grounds. I know it is impossible, of course.'

'Not at all,' I said, seized by a sudden boldness. 'It's no problem.'

'But how?' he asked

'I can go in and sign the visitors' book.'

In those pre-terrorist days, it was possible for members of the public to walk in through the front gate and go on into the Palace, to the room where a visitor's book was kept. I told him, 'Just make sure you stand well back, near the Victoria Statue. I just want to go in and out as quickly as possible, and I don't want anyone to spot the camera. Photograph me all you want, but don't get spotted.'

So I walked up to the policeman at the gate, making sure I kept my head down and my face slightly averted, and said I wanted to go in to sign the visitors' book.

He said with a little smile, 'Haven't I seen you somewhere before?'

'Oh, no, I don't think so,' I said and strode in. I walked into the special room to one side of the Palace, guarded by an official. He escorted me to the huge, leather-bound book where I dutifully wrote my name and address then walked out.

Walking out, aware that the camera would be trained on me, I straightened my shoulders and stepped out of the gate very smartly. I smiled at the policeman and, would you believe it, he saluted me! It made an astonishing picture which I believe was syndicated all over the world. The editor and his photographer were as pleased as punch. When I got back to them, a crowd of Commonwealth citizens gathered around us and they got some fine photographs there to complete their day.

A bunch of models looked fabulous and attracted a large crowd around the Victoria Statue when I worked there on an assignment for the German fashion magazine, *Journal*. The idea was to convey the impression that the Queen had strolled out from the Palace to inspect the models. The photographer had obtained a permit from the Lord Chamberlain's office to use the pavement near the Palace, and the afternoon tourists milled around taking a great interest in what was going on.

It was a very cold day, and I sheltered in a car until I was called on to step into the shot. I must say I felt sorry for the girls who had to wait around in their flimsy dresses while the photographer completed his preparations. A couple of policemen walked over, shook hands with me, and had a chuckle at the scene we were setting up.

The flag was flying over the Palace, the sign that the Queen is in residence, and I wondered if she ever came to the windows to have a look at what was going on outside. If she had looked out on that day, she would have seen not only the models but a huge contingent of tourists from China who all seemed to have a photograph taken with me.

I once posed in a car being driven down the Mall for some students from a girls' college who wanted to take photographs for a competition. They got a beautiful picture of me looking out of the back window, with Buckingham Palace in the background. They won the competition, and I got a great deal of pleasure from helping a group of enthusiastic youngsters.

A commercial for Ritters, a German brand of chocolates, had me walking around St James's Park. A hazard of this particular assignment was that the planned photograph called for me to take a bite from a newly opened bar, and the cameraman wanted to take a lot of shots to make sure he got it right. It was beautiful chocolate but after many, many bites, I was heartily sick of it. By the time I had finished the long session, a crowd of children who had gathered to watch came over to collect a mountain of chocolate bars, all with one bite missing.

I could not help wondering what tourists must have thought when I posed with Buckingham Palace for backdrop with Paul King, the lead singer with The King group. The theme of the promotion photographs, taken for the music trade press, was the King meeting the Queen. Paul King's trade mark is psychedelic boots so I put on a similar pair and Paul and I were photographed walking across the road wearing them. It was a terrific idea, and, with my being so short anyway, I looked hilarious in the boots.

A piece of Buckingham Palace filming for an American television company might have caused an international incident. The cameras were set up at a discreet distance by the Victoria Statue, trained on me as I walked across the road to draw reactions. We got one I hadn't expected.

A senior police officer, a truly charming gentleman, came up to me, shook my hand, and said, 'I do know who you are, and I'm delighted to meet you. My wife will be delighted, too, because she is a great admirer of yours. But I must point out two things. First, you need the Lord Chamberlain's permission to film here. Second, we have President Giscard d'Estaing inside the Palace at the moment, and he's due out soon. I think he would be quite shocked if he left Her Majesty inside and came out to see you here.'

He had a very good point, and I beat a hasty retreat in the interest of international relations and whatever might have been left of the *Entente Cordiale*. But the crew filming me were delighted with this incident because they managed to get pictures of me being greeted near the Palace gates by an obviously very senior police officer. It was a definite bonus, and was shown in the finished film.

I've always got on well with the police around the Palace, and over the years I've become a familiar face to them. Whenever they've had cause to come over to me because, perhaps, a crowd has gathered, I've always made a point of shaking hands and introducing myself. After all, it costs nothing to be polite.

There have been a number of occasions when such a large crowd has gathered the police have had to ask me to duck out of the way to give it an incentive to disperse. I've always been co-operative about this but I'm not sure which is worse: for a big crowd to gather and get in the way, or for no one to notice me at all. And I always have to be on my best behaviour, whatever strain the director's or cameraman's request has placed me under.

Of course, the star treatment that results from my line of work has its advantages. It can be very nice to have commissionaires rushing to open doors for me, or offering to park my car. Some people pretend to mistake me for the Queen, like the policeman who spotted me carrying my suitcase of equipment to a wedding reception near the Mall.

'Would you like an escort down to the Palace, ma'am?'

'No thank you, not on this occasion,' I replied.

When I had delivered my speech, another policeman was waiting outside to ask if he could have a photograph taken with me. I agreed but he didn't have a camera with him, of course, so I had to put down my suitcase, open it up, take out my camera and get someone to take the picture for us. All on top of a full working day!

'It's fun what you do, isn't it?' he said blithely.

'Yes,' I replied, 'if it wasn't, I wouldn't do it.'

'Well, carry on with the good work,' he said with a nice little salute.

Less friendly was a conductor on a bus near Trafalgar Square when I got on, wearing a beautiful green outfit, so that a photographer working for *Neue Revue*, a German magazine, could take pictures of me on the platform. We told him what we were doing, and only wanted to go one stop. He said he didn't care what we were doing, we'd have to pay. In fact, he threatened to stop the bus if we didn't. He said, 'It doesn't matter who you are. If you were the Queen herself, you'd still have to pay.'

I returned to the Royal Academy in Piccadilly some years after my 'discovery' to view a painting called 'The White Hat', an exhibit at the Summer Exhibition, in which the subject bore a striking resemblance to Princess Anne. It was earmarked to become the prize in a competition organised by the *Daily Mirror*, and I was taken along to the Academy to stand by the painting so photographers could record people's reactions to the sight. I got quite a few quizzical stares, and I believe a few people thought the Queen had popped in to see the painting.

When people do pluck up the courage to directly approach me, the results can be rather funny. An American boy who spotted me in The Silver Vaults in Chancery Lane asked me if I would send his grandmother a birthday telegram when she was a hundred. I asked how old his grandmother was and it turned out she was some years younger than me so I told him, 'When your Granny is closer to a hundred, write to Buckingham Palace and you'll most likely receive an answer.'

A television appearance at a West End club with Janet Street-Porter was nicely rounded off when I walked out of it to find a very pleasant middle-aged lady waiting for me. 'Madam, are you allowed to receive presents?' she asked.

I laughed. 'Yes, I am, thank you very much. Why? Have you got something for me?' She said 'yes' and gave me a small spray of flowers. I thanked her and walked off, sure she thought I was the Queen.

I do believe it's sometimes kinder not to disillusion people, particularly if they are children. I can remember when I myself learned there was no Father Christmas, and it came as an awful shock to me. I remembered that when a lady came over to me in a supermarket and said to me, 'I'm sure you're Mrs Charles, though you are so like the Queen. But I'm sure the Queen would not shop here.' She hesitated for a moment then asked, 'You're not her by any chance, are you?' I said I was not, and she continued, 'Would you please just talk to my children?'

I went over to the two children, who were aged about five and eight, had a little talk with them then walked very quickly away. If those children thought they had seen the Queen and I told them otherwise, it would have spoiled their day. Now they'll go through life believing they met the Queen, and what a lovely childhood memory that will be.

An elderly Australian lady came up to me one day when I was in London doing some shopping and said, 'My dear, I know who you are. I've seen you on television. I've spent all my money to come to London to see Princess Anne get married, and perhaps catch a glimpse of the royal family.'

I think she knew I was Jeannette Charles, but my appearance certainly fooled a very sweet old couple who first looked behind me as if expecting to see my security guards then said, 'We're awfully embarrassed at stopping you, but we do love you so.'

A television studio is not the place where I expect this sort of mistake to take place, but it certainly did when a rather urbane old gentleman came up to me and said, 'My dear, you look absolutely charming today. How have you been, and how is your mother, and your sister?' I thought it was rather odd because I'd never met the man before. He had certainly mistaken me for somebody else. Then he said, 'Thank you for your invitation, and I'd be delighted. I will be accepting.' When he had gone, I asked someone who the man was, and it turned out to be the writer, J. Wentworth Day, who, so I hear, was on very close terms with the royal family.

A studio of a different kind held a surprise for me when I went along to have some fun photographs taken by the *Sun*. I was to be dressed in my regalia and an oversize crown which slipped down over my face. I went into the changing room at the photographic studio, and as I opened the door an absolutely beautiful girl was standing there completely starkers. It was Jilly Johnson, the famous Page Three model. I was stunned but managed to keep my cool and say, 'I'm so sorry, I was coming in to change.'

Jilly was completely unembarrassed. 'Hello, Jeannette, I'm very pleased to meet you,' she said, shaking my hand formally. 'Give me a moment, and the room will be yours.'

I was walking across Wardour Street in Soho to take some clothes into a dry cleaner's when an Indian or Pakistani gentleman spotted me, put his arm by his side and stood rigidly to attention. He stared at me and after me till I was out of sight. There's no doubt in my mind that he thought he had spotted the Queen walking by.

A stallholder in Petticoat Lane was less certain when I visited him on a walkabout for a magazine. He said, 'I know you. Princess Margaret, aren't you?' But he later told a reporter, 'Of course, I knew it was the Queen.' A man selling patriotic souvenirs thought his dream had come true, and executed a beautiful bow when I walked up to his stall. A pearly king looked shocked and said, 'I know your face, don't I? No, it can't be. Not down the Lane.'

I can stroll unnoticed in a crowd, but a sudden incident can change all that. Take the time I was walking down a street when I saw a woman knocked down by a car. She wasn't seriously injured but I made her as comfortable as possible and saw her into an ambulance. At first she could not see my face but when she spotted it as I said goodbye, she just about fainted.

One evening, my daughter, Carol, was driving me through London on my way to an engagement when I had to get out to ask directions from a man. He looked at me, then furtively behind me, then backed away. 'Oh, no,' he said. 'Oh, no!' He looked around again, and by this time Carol was roaring with laughter. 'Oh, no!' he repeated. 'This must be "Candid Camera".' He turned tail and ran off up the street.

I had an uncomfortable moment myself when I went to the first night of the film 'Coal Miner's Daughter' with my husband. Afterwards we went to a party organised for the première's guests. Anybody who was anybody in British showbusiness was there. We filled our plates with food from the buffet, turned into the crowd to look for a seat, and as we did so I came eyeball to eyeball with Roddy Llewellyn, the man who gained short-lived notoriety a few years ago as escort to Princess Margaret. Eyeball to eyeball is precisely right because he is no bigger than me. We stared at each other for a few seconds until I said, 'Excuse me, can I come past you?' He stepped to one side, and I walked past him. For some reason, I was extremely embarrassed. He just looked bemused.

My looks have at times proved a great help when it comes to dealing with traffic wardens, like the day I was chauffeured into London in a Rolls-Royce and the driver parked near the Grosvenor House Hotel. A lady traffic warden came walking up with her pad and pen at the ready. Then she spotted me, and looked, and looked. I stepped out, smiled at her, and walked into the hotel. When I glanced back she was chatting with the chauffeur, and he told me later she'd said, 'Oh, dear, I can't give Her Majesty a ticket, can I?'

Nearby Hyde Park was the scene of my encounter with two more lady traffic wardens. I was in a caravan changing room parked close to the Serpentine, preparing for a sketch for the Jim Davidson show. I could hear the wardens talking to the producer, and one of them telling him, 'You're on a yellow line and it's illegal to park here. There is a place further down where you can park a caravan.'

I stepped out clad in my full regalia and what a conversation stopper that was! One of the wardens said, 'Jesus Christ, here's the Queen!' Then we explained and had a talk and a laugh about it. Instead of giving us a ticket, both the girls asked for my autograph.

A German television crew who parked a limousine outside the Tower of London were also about to get a ticket from yet another lady warden, who was approaching menacingly as we came out from a visit to the Tower when I boldly told the crew, 'I'll take care of this.' I went straight up to the girl, put my hand out, and said, 'Hello, my dear, nice to see you.' She looked shaken but recovered enough to start giving us a lecture about parking there. Then she laughed and walked off without giving us a ticket.

A call to a photographer's studio in trendily refurbished Covent Garden nearly had me bumping into Prince Philip. I was looking around a converted warehouse, searching for the studio, when I heard a voice say, 'Cor blimey, it's her!' Then a man nudged my arm and said, 'Hey, missus, aren't you supposed to be over there?'

I looked to where he was pointing and, to my embarrassment, Prince Philip was standing there with a group of people. I said to the man, 'You must be kidding.'

He looked puzzled then said, 'You're not 'er then?'

'What do you mean?'

'You know, 'er Majesty.'

'I'm the lady who's supposed to look like the Queen,' I explained.

'Gor' blimey, I can't believe it, I *don't* believe it,' he said.

My route to the studio should have taken me very close to where Prince Philip was standing, but I could not bring myself to pass him by. Instead, I ducked in the other direction, got there by almost going round the block, and made sure Prince Philip had moved on before I scurried into the studio.

I also almost ran into the Queen one day when I arrived at Liverpool Street Station, the London terminus for my local line. As I got off the train, I spotted a crowd and worked my way through to the front to see what was attracting all the attention. And there was the Queen, walking along shaking hands. For a moment I wanted to get into place for a handshake, then I remembered how I'd nearly collapsed during our earlier confrontation at the end of my street so I switched course to cross to another part of the station.

A stranger experience at the same station involved a well-dressed man in a morning suit who started making a point of stopping me and introducing me to travellers around us. In those days, I used to go back and forth by train quite often, and my encounters with this man began when he greeted me off a train one day by saying, 'Very nice to see you, Mrs Charles.'

He was really charming and polite, but it soon got that every time I arrived at the station he'd be there to welcome me, insisting on taking me for a coffee in the buffet and drawing other people over to talk to me. Once he met me and said, 'There's a couple here who've come from Birmingham and I told them you were due on the train. They are fans of yours, and they'd like to meet you. I'd like you to meet them.' So he took me to see the couple and we all had tea together.

I don't to this day know how he learnt which train I'd be arriving on. Perhaps he had a spy at Chelmsford who kept him informed. Eventually I grew to resent his proprietorial behaviour and resorted to wearing a wig to disguise myself from him. Whenever I came into the station, I'd try to creep round him to get out to the taxi rank before he could claim me.

There was also a girl who always seemed to appear on whatever train I was using, and make a point of having a talk with me.

Then there was the time that I reached the station on my way home late at night after an engagement. I heard footsteps pounding after me, and there was this very scary gang of punks bearing down on me. I thought I was about to be mugged and was scared silly. I was about to surrender my handbag when one of them asked for my autograph! I've never been so pleased to give it.

Mistaken identity has never been so much fun as the time I left a personal appearance engagement in Soho. A limousine was waiting for me, and two motorbike officers were parked in front of it. I thought they were going to present me with a parking ticket but when they saw me, dressed in a lovely blue outfit and hat, the officers snapped off smart salutes. Of course, the fact that the car had numberplates with HRH 1 might also have had something to do with it.

The chauffeur opened the door for me, the motorcyclist took up position as outriders, and we were off. I had intended to go to my agent's office to change but, instead I whispered to the driver 'Liverpool Street Station', and he took me there. It was a fabulous journey, and I could see that people along the way thought it was a royal car under escort. We whizzed through the traffic in no time at all. Isn't it amazing how cars will pull over to let an escorted vehicle through? At Liverpool Street Station I got out, shook hands with my chauffeur, then went round to the motorcyclists and shook hands with them.

I said, 'Thank you very much, fellows. I'm off home now.' They didn't mind at all, and thought it was all very funny. I had to suffer a journey home as the centre of attention in all my finery, but that escorted drive through town was worth it.

There wasn't really much danger of my being mistaken for the Queen as I walked through the City of London on the day Prince Charles and Lady Diana were married at St Paul's Cathedral. After all, everybody knew exactly where she was that day.

We had a flat in the Barbican at that time, and Ken woke me up to ask if I wanted to have a stroll through to St Paul's to watch the events of the day. I'd arrived back from an appearance in Wales just a few hours before and was exhausted but I hauled myself up because I knew the wedding was a sight not to be missed.

On our way, people called out to me and waved. One man said, 'Shouldn't you be in the cathedral?' There was a marvellous atmosphere in the City that day. A policeman riding by on horseback patted the rump of his horse and asked, 'Would you like to sit up here?' I said, 'No, thank you,' so he asked, 'What about an escort then?' 'No, I think I'll manage,' said I. It was a lovely, lovely day, with people coming up to talk to me, happy and joking. I had no intention of standing along the main road where perhaps the Queen or other members of the royal family might see me. Ken and I found a spot in a side street near St Paul's, and managed to get a glimpse of the procession.

Of course, I had received a number of invitations to participate in photo sessions connected to the wedding, but they all came from foreign magazines who were interested in using me to sensationalise the event. I turned them all down flat.

I did accept another invitation in the same year, to Chelmsford Crown Court for a stint of jury service. I went into a waiting room with the other prospective jurors and became the focus of attention for a bunch of staring strangers, all nudging each other and whispering. I tried to read a newspaper and ignore it, then someone broke the ice by coming over to say, 'Aren't you the lady who impersonates the Queen on television?'

When it was my turn to enter the courtroom, the prisoner pointed to me and said, 'That lady's face looks very familiar. I don't think I want her on my jury.' The judge and the clerk of the court were both grinning and I was asked to stand down. When I filed into another of the courts, the young man in the dock looked at me and smiled as if to say: 'Lovely to have you on my side.'

It does amuse me when people who spot me out in the street whistle the National Anthem or 'Land of Hope and Glory' to let me know they've recognised me. I am much less comfortable about the furtive watchers who follow me around stores. Once they latch on to me, every time I stop at a counter there they are, peeking again. I've often abandoned shopping expeditions because of this. I've tried putting on hats, scarves, or dark glasses to hide from inquisitive gazes but that sort of disguise often attracts its own form of attention.

The train journeys into London became a particular trial. Wherever I sat, I'd find someone staring at me. Either that, or total strangers would strike up conversations with me. The journey lasts forty minutes and they would want to talk all the way. I'm a shy and very private person, and I find it difficult to handle conversations like this. I mean, what do you say to a total stranger for that length of time?

Even when my daughter and I made a day trip flight on Concorde it was ruined by people crowding around and asking for my autograph.

The result of all this is that I've had to abandon travelling on public transport. I have to drive around to all my engagements by car which can be very tiring but at least it affords me the privacy I need. Carol is a little gem, and whenever she can she drives me around the country to my various jobs.

A much pleasanter aspect of my career is the number of friends it has brought me all over the world. Many of them come to visit me, and I visit them when I'm off on my travels. I also get letters from all over the world from people who have seen me in advertisements or on television shows. I call this my 'royal mail', and letters addressed just to 'Jeannette Charles, England' have reached me. The people who write – and some even telephone from as far away as Canada – seem to share my views on the royals and are glad that an ordinary person like me can express their feelings on the subject publicly.

There is also a sinister side to this public recognition. Very early in my 'second career' I answered the telephone at home to hear a cultured man's voice say, 'We're going to kill you.' That was all he said, then he hung up. There was no malice in his tone. He just spoke matter-of-factly, which made it seem even more threatening. At first I was stunned, then I started shivering. The telephone rang again and there was the same even voice: 'We're going to kill you.'

When I regained my composure I called my husband at his office, and he came straight home. I contacted the police who came round to investigate. They asked where the children were at school, and arranged to keep an eye on them. Our telephone was monitored and the house was fitted with all sorts of anti-intruder devices like pressure pads and alarms.

It was an awful time for me, and I became scared to step outside the house. I called off all my work engagements, and in fact I didn't go back to work for six months. The police explained that anybody who gets a lot of publicity is liable to have this sort of thing happen. It also occurred to me that kidnappers might grab me and use it as a warning of what they could do to royalty. When the kidnap attempt was made on Princess Anne in the The Mall, it got me to thinking that someone might kidnap me in mistake for the Queen. The IRA attacks around London have made me particularly alert if I ever use stores the Queen is known to visit. Remember that a lot of people are genuinely confused about whether or not I am the Queen. So you'll never find me strolling down a street window shopping. And if I visit the lady's room at an airport or somewhere else, I always make sure there are plenty of other people around in there first. There must be less chance of anything happening if other people are present.

I am so impressed with the way the Queen, despite the ever present threat of danger, will move around freely and close to crowds. Because of my own experiences, I know how nerve-racking it can be. I think she is very courageous.

I was once followed by a car when I was being driven in a Rolls-Royce from my home to Wembley for an engagement. The driver had to take us at speed round side streets to lose our pursuer. I'll never know if it was merely a curious spectator following us, or someone with a much darker purpose.

During my days of travelling by train I had another unpleasant experience. I was heading back to London from an engagement in Maidstone when a very odd-looking man seated himself opposite me. All the way he stared intently at me but said not a word. I was terrified, and when we reached the station I ran as fast as I could to a taxi.

Despite my fears, if the Queen's security people ever wanted me to step in to act as her double in a particular situation which they considered hazardous for Her Majesty, I would do it. I haven't been asked to do this yet, but the possibility has obviously occurred to others. I vividly recall a cartoon in the *London Evening News* which depicted the Queen reading a newspaper with the headline 'Queen's Visit to Zambia Unsafe'. A worried-looking Prince Philip was reading over her shoulder, and the caption read, 'What's that woman's name who does those rather good impersonations of me on the telly?'

I was, however, called to stand in for the Queen when a sculptress was making a bust of Her Majesty for The Queen's Theatre in Hornchurch, not too many miles from my home. The sculptress, Dorothy Russell, had written to Buckingham Palace to ask if the Queen could sit for her, but was told that her schedule of engagements made it impossible.

Mrs Russell had read about me in a newspaper, and asked me to sit for her instead. Apparently working from a live model is particularly important when modelling the forehead and cheeks. The bust of 'the Queen' outside the theatre in Hornchurch is really me.

CHAPTER EIGHT

Around the World

It was a monumental spoof, even for the Monty Python crowd. I made an entrance at the Cannes Film Festival and an agency report appeared on teleprinters around the world: 'The Queen makes a surprise visit.'

The Australian press contingent were so taken in that they called a meeting to decide which one had the smartest suit and was presentable enough to be introduced to Her Majesty at a rapidly arranged screening put on in her honour!

I had been hired to help promote 'Monty Python and the Holy Grail', and in the days leading up to the festival *Cinema TV* magazine carried an advertisement announcing that 'a very gracious lady' would attend a showing of the Holy Grail film for overseas buyers.

I flew over to Nice Airport where Eric Idle and other members of the Monty Python team scooped me up and rushed me through the terminal and into a waiting car.

They took me to the hotel in Cannes where I was told the 'British delegation' was awaiting me. I was introduced to a teenage girl and left with her.

'Shall I go and get washed and dressed and changed for the British delegation?' I asked her.

'Oh, no,' she said. 'It's me.'

'What do you mean, it's you?'

'I am the British delegation.'

I was rather taken aback. 'But you're only one person,' I pointed out.

She shrugged her shoulders and said, 'Well, that's Monty Python for you.'

We had a good laugh and lunch together before the Monty Python guys came back to escort me into the festival exhibition room, which was in another hotel a short distance away.

I was dressed in a two-piece cream silk suit and a pretty hat as I walked in surrounded by my phalanx of Monty Python escorts: Eric Idle, Graham Chapman, Neil Innes, Terry Gilliam, and John Goldstone, their producer. I moved along very sedately, nodding my head in greeting to people on either side who were manning the stands set up by their various film companies. People stopped talking in mid-conversation, others stood to attention. I gave a little wave here, a smile there. We walked right on into the section where journalists reporting the festival sat at banks of typewriters, hammering out their pieces. One by one, the journalists looked up, stopped typing and started rising to their feet. It was so funny I was laughing inside but, wearing my most serious expression, I left the press room and returned to the exhibition where I stopped at the occasional stand to talk to exhibitors and shake hands. Then we all turned to walk slowly back through the hall, out of the hotel, and I was taken back to the car to be driven back to my hotel.

I changed later into a summer frock and took a walk around the terrace of the hotel where I met a host of V.I.P. visitors, and actors and actresses. So many people gave me their cards that by the end of the afternoon my handbag was bulging with them. Then I was taken with my Monty Python entourage along the Cannes promenade where for a short while I distracted the men's attention from the rows of naked girls who were covering the beach.

In the evening, I dressed in a beautiful evening gown and jewellery and was driven to one of the hotels where the festival's films are shown. I stepped out on to a red carpet and was blinded by the light of scores of camera flashes. I walked in, again flanked by the Monty Python group. We made our unhurried way up the stairs for a grand entrance to the theatre. People were clapping and cheering and crowding around to get a look. I settled into my seat, the lights were lowered for the première of 'Monty Python and the Holy Grail', and I fell immediately and soundly asleep!

I remember being pushed and nudged and pinched to stay awake but I couldn't at the end of what had been a very long day. Fortunately it was too dark for most people to notice but I heard Terry Gilliam say to Eric Idle, 'Well, she's finished for the evening. We'd better take her back to the hotel.' They did, and I collapsed into my bed for a sound and very long sleep.

This trip to the Côte d'Azur, and the excitement of attending an international film festival, was just one of the many lovely bonuses of my 'second career'. I have always loved travelling, and my work has taken me to more parts of the world than I ever thought I would see.

I've been back to America, where I worked as a young woman, on many occasions. It's always been great fun, though I am sometimes daunted by the scale of things there.

I got the full star treatment in Los Angeles, where I compèred a most amazing and extravagant fashion show at the Beverley Hills Hotel. I was billed as 'the well-known actress', a title I didn't really deserve. The Royal Gala Ball in Chicago was a glittering event in a magnificently decorated room at the Hilton International Hotel. I came in after the food and along with the cigars to deliver a speech from the centre of a giant horseshoe table at one end of the room. The reception could not, surely, have been bettered if I *had* been the Queen, and I enjoyed the full blast of the famous Chicago hospitality. People who spoke to me afterwards as I walked around said they were fed up with waiting in the cold to see famous people such as President Reagan, and catching just a glimpse of them as they sped by in a car. It was so nice, they said, to be able to inspect me at leisure and in the warm.

Las Vegas is the show capital of America, and I had the pleasure of going to an assignment to Caesar's Palace Hotel, which is what a Roman palace would have looked like if only the emperors could have afforded it! I was dressed in my full regalia, complete with tiara, and introduced as 'a very special lady'. I had been provided with a speech to read to delegates from the Bell Telephone Company and their wives. The convention's organisers had handed me the script earlier, and given me some very old-fashioned looks when I said I wanted to alter it to include some of my own dialogue.

As I delivered my speech the Master of Ceremonies, who was sitting next to me, interrupted me so much that I finally had to tell him, in a very severe voice, 'Sir! I am not used to interruptions.' The room fell absolutely silent, and he went beetroot red. But it worked. He didn't say another word. When I had finished, I walked around the room, shaking hands, and I swear to this day that because of the way I had called the Master of Ceremonies into line, many of the delegates thought I *was* the Queen.

Quite a crowd had gathered outside the room, and Jaki Baskow, an agent who handles my Las Vegas bookings, urged me, 'Take a walk around the casino.'

'No, I don't think that would be right,' I said. I was very conscious of the tiara and other trappings I was wearing.

'Oh, it's all right here – this is Las Vegas, anything goes,' Jaki reassured me.

'All right, but only round the casino.'

I walked slowly round a huge room which was packed with hundreds of people playing slot machines. A lot of people actually stopped playing to stare at me. They didn't make a sound, just stared. There was an electric atmosphere in the room as the gamblers stood stock still. The Queen must be greatly respected out there because it takes a lot to distract the dedicated gamblers of Las Vegas from their slot machines.

I noticed a group of men following us, and they turned out to be reporters from the Las Vegas newspapers. They cornered Jaki to ask her, 'Do you think Her Majesty would have a word with us?' Jaki told them gravely, 'No, I'm sorry. Her Majesty *never* gives interviews.' Later an item appeared in one of the city's newspapers saying that the Queen had secretly visited Las Vegas.

Jaki had an open car, and she offered to drive me up and down the Las Vegas Strip, the neon-lit highway where all the city's main hotels are located. I refused the offer. Playing a rôle in the hotel, even in the casino, was one thing but flaunting myself in a vulgar way along the Strip was something else.

However, while I was in the gambling capital of the world, I wanted to try my luck. I asked one of the hotel staff, 'Can you help me make some money from the slot machines?' He pointed one out to me and said, 'If you keep having a go at that one, you'll have a win. People have been feeding it all night and it hasn't paid up yet this evening.' I tackled that machine and won £25.

My adviser then said: 'Your face is your fortune. You could really make some money. There's a wonderful restaurant which is to open up here very soon, and if you like I will recommend you for a job there. You can sit in the window and attract attention.'

'That's very kind of you, but I have work already and I do have a home to go to,' I said.

'Pity, it would be very nice to have you here in Las Vegas.'

I didn't think so, though. Just sitting in a restaurant window would have been so boring.

It was Jaki who arranged for me to go to the opening of another restaurant unlike anything I have ever seen. It was owned by that extrovert American legend, Liberace. The establishment was due to be opened a few days later, and Lee (as Liberace is known to his family and friends) was to launch it with an invitation-only guest night. Family and friends were invited, along with a lot of people who had worked on refurbishing the restaurant, such as the architect and designer. Jaki told Liberace's sister-in-law, Dora, that I was in town and she was excited to hear it for Liberace had been in London to play at a soirée given by the Queen at Buckingham Palace only a few days before. 'You must bring Jeannette along,' Dora told Jaki.

So, on the opening night, Ken and I went to the restaurant, accompanied by Jaki and her husband. Liberace came over to greet us, gave me a big hug and said, 'Jeannette, I've just left the Queen in London. It's like greeting Her Majesty all over again.'

We were introduced to Liberace's brother, George, and his sister, Angie, an astonishing little lady who is in her seventies yet still runs a trucking company, and can get up and drive the vehicles if necessary.

The main room of the restaurant had a ceiling painted silver and the tables were laid with the most beautiful silverware and crystal. I thought they must have equipped the restaurant like that just for the gala evening, but apparently it was to be like that always. The tables were of glass so clear it was practically invisible. All the guests were seated four to a table round the edge of the room but Liberace sat and ate on his own at a table in the centre. Every once in a while someone would go over to give him a kiss or shake his hand and congratulate him.

The restaurant was an amazing place – it hardly felt as if it was the real world at all. There was also a baroque room, a German room, and a Chinese room, where the furniture and fitments all faithfully matched the chosen theme.

Later in the evening, Lee stood to make a little speech. He said, 'I'd like you all to meet a special guest, a lady who has come all the way from England, a lady who is so much like the Queen, whom I left in London only last week, that I just feel we've got Her Majesty with us tonight.'

He gave out a series of gifts to people who had helped in setting up the restaurant, then called me up to the microphone, made a big fuss of me, and got me to present an enormous bottle of champagne to a girl from his accountant's office who had made a special contribution.

We were entertained by a fashion show with models circulating among the tables, by an opera singer, and by a ballet dancer, yet the atmosphere was so convivial that I still felt part of a happy family gathering.

When it was time for me to go, Liberace said he hoped perhaps to see me in London, and asked me to go the following morning to the Liberace Museum, which was close by. So, at the appointed time, Jaki and I turned up at the museum to be met by Dora and George. Dora runs the museum, and it was easy to see how proud she was of that astonishing place.

The museum is like a palace. We entered through huge doors and were led up a great staircase to view the exhibits. In a collection of memorabilia of the Liberace family there are photographs and letters on display, illustrating the children's growth into adulthood. Lee is the youngest and was a child prodigy, playing the piano when he was only three years old.

There is also a piano on display which was owned by Liszt, another which belonged to Chopin, and an enormous limousine painted red, white, and blue in commemoration of the American Bicentennial year of 1976.

I got a big hug from George, and Dora said, 'We've got something for you.' A secretary brought over a big box. 'Lee wanted us to give you a present to take back to England.' Inside the box was a china ornament in the shape of a piano with a candelabra. It is now in the sitting-room of my home.

Canada is also a country I'd known previously, and I was delighted to be invited back there to spend a couple of weeks working on promotions in Vancouver, way over on the Pacific coast. I was not so happy when I arrived at the airport to be told that my work visa had not been arranged. I was told to wait by the immigration office, and people kept coming up to a window to take a look at me. It made me feel as if I was in a fish bowl.

I'd arrived late at night, and when an hour had passed like this I was feeling tired and very irritated. I called to one of the officials, 'Could you tell me, please, exactly what is going on?'

'I know who you are,' he said, 'but even if you were the Queen herself, you'd have to wait.'

I was under the mistaken impression that British subjects were Canadian citizens, and vice versa. Not any more, apparently, which gave me quite a shock. I suggested I be sent to a hotel where I could get some sleep and that I would go home the next day.

Finally, the man responsible for arranging my stay turned up and the visa problem was resolved. The immigration official I had seen earlier came out to say, 'We're terribly sorry, Mrs Charles, but we can't go against regulations.' After that slightly ignominious start, I was taken to a lovely hotel penthouse which was big enough for four people. Flowers were waiting for me, and the service was first class.

A number of different stores and other organisations had collaborated to pay my fee and expenses, and to advertise my appearance on the local radio station. I spent most of my time at an enormous furniture store talking to prospective customers.

I remember one man had heard on the radio that I was in town so he dashed home from work and raced over on his bicycle to see me before the store closed. He was so much out of breath and in such a state of high excitement when he arrived that I got a member of the store's staff to make him a cup of tea to help calm him down.

I also appeared at a waxworks exhibition where I would stand at the door to greet people. On one occasion I sat on a seat in front of an effigy of the Queen, so immobile that some people thought I was a waxwork model. As a woman walked in, I just happened to stand up. She staggered in surprise and I thought she was going to faint.

I've been on trips to Singapore to address delegates attending the Asian Advertising Congress and, on another occasion, over a thousand representatives of Singapore Airlines from all over the world. It's a wonderful experience to enter a vast auditorium and have everybody there rise to their feet in spontaneous welcome. I know exactly how Her Majesty must feel in similar circumstances.

Singapore is one of the most fascinating parts of the world that I've ever been to, and, of course, I always stay at Raffles Hotel there. That's another bonus of my lookalike globetrotting, having my first-class fares and bills in the world's most renowned hotels paid for me.

My V.I.P. status was, however, not enough to gain me admittance to the First Class lounge on a Qantas 747 flight taking me to an assignment in Australia. I was travelling First Class and after we had been in the air a few hours I wanted to go up to the lounge, the area contained in the 'hump' at the front of the plane, to sit down, have a drink, and perhaps do some writing. I was stopped by a steward at the bottom of the stairs.

'I'm sorry, madam,' he said. 'You can't go up there.'

'Why on earth not?' I asked. 'This is First Class, and it's the First Class lounge.'

'Madam, I'm very embarrassed about this, and it's very awkward for us, but Princess Margaret is up there.'

'Well, that's fine,' I said. 'Princess Margaret has obviously got a First Class seat, too.'

'It's not quite like that,' said the steward. 'She told the Captain that she and her entourage wanted to take over the lounge for the whole of the flight, and she won't allow anyone else up there.'

'Surely that's not right,' I protested. 'The First Class lounge is for all the First Class passengers.'

'What can I say?' the steward said with a shrug. 'Unfortunately, there is nothing we can do about it.'

The Princess and her party apparently came downstairs just before we landed at Sydney. I did not see her, but if I had I would have felt tempted to tell her that she had not behaved very generously.

No matter what you've heard about the Australians' republicanism, they are fascinated by our royal family. Some, certainly, think they are outdated and archaic but there's a great deal of love for them, too, although all Australians are fiercely proud to be Australians. I seem to be popping over there all the time, and I've met Australians in just about every part of their country so I have a good idea how they feel.

I am regularly flown over there by syndicates of businessmen promoting huge suburban shopping malls built at the centre of industrial and private housing developments. The first of these took me early in my career to an outlying Sydney location where I walked around each day giving out raffle tickets, signing autographs, and generally making myself visible.

I stayed in the centre of Sydney, at the Sebel Town House Hotel, which has a lobby as high as a cathedral. I was given champagne, fruit and flowers, and put up in a glorious penthouse which is usually reserved for the Queen, Presidents, or other heads of state.

A particularly fond memory of this trip concerns a young man I met when I stepped out of the hotel to get some air. He rushed up to me like a whirlwind, he was so excited. 'I'm absolutely delighted to meet you,' he enthused. 'I've seen you on television and read about you. I think it's great, really marvellous.' He gushed on and on, without pausing for breath. I felt quite overwhelmed. Then he whipped off his V-neck cream and red cricket sweater and held it out to me. 'Please take this as a present,' he said.

'I couldn't possibly,' I protested.

'Yes, you can,' he said. 'I'm the captain of the cricket team, and I want you to have it as a gift. I haven't got anything else to give you, and I may not see you again. My wife knitted it, and she'll be really knocked out that you've got it.'

I brought the sweater home and Carol loved it so much that she commandeered it and has worn it to college a great deal.

At the shopping mall, where I was also filmed walking in and out of the shops, a lady in charge of a leather boutique said to me, 'I wish we could keep you here. We've always loved the royal family, my family and I, and it would be so marvellous if you lived here.' She was a sweet woman and insisted on giving me a beautiful leather handbag as a momento of my visit.

To top this venture, I was filmed being driven in a Rolls-Royce and taking tea in a courtyard garden before being perched on a velvet chair to intone a Christmas and New Year message extolling the virtues of the shopping mall to the television viewers of Sydney.

I also travelled to Sydney's southern rival, Melbourne, to don my tiara and watch the world première of the film 'The Great McCarthy', an epic about Australian rules football which seems to be a cross between mayhem and murder. I appeared in the 'royal box' of the Athenaeum Theatre, and got a thunderous reception.

I seemed to be on every radio news programme around, and my filmed appearances at the mall attracted so many cheering, waving people and so much publicity that my working future in Australia was assured.

I have been on countless chat shows 'down under', and whenever I have been in Australia and a David Frost show is in the offing, I have been invited to appear on it. I've always found David Frost a very direct interviewer, easy to talk to, and he's always been willing to sit back and let me express my point of view.

The Australian interviewers are somewhat more abrasive, and with them I've often found myself acting as unofficial ambassadress for the Queen, a rôle which has become second nature to me over the years.

What particularly surprised me about the Australian interviewers was how they assumed that because I look like the Queen, I actually have close contact with the royal family.

Whenever I have returned for shopping mall promotions, the questions have continued. About the Queen, the Queen Mother, about Prince Charles, Princess Anne and Mark Phillips, and, of course, about Margaret Thatcher. Those about our lady Prime Minister are probably the most difficult for me because I'm not the most well-informed person about politics. All I know is what I read and hear on radio or television so I just have to hope that most of it is true.

Perth, in the far west of Australia, is very different from the heavily populated east coast. Scratch the surface around Sydney or Melbourne and you'll find a lot of anti-royalists. Perth, on the other hand, has many people who have arrived from Britain comparatively recently, a lot of them retired industrial workers from our northern counties, and they, of course, could not imagine being without the Queen.

I have carried out similar shopping mall promotions around there and it has been touching to be approached by elderly gentlemen wanting to talk to me about their time in the last war, or to tell me, perhaps, that they met King George VI.

My promotions there have often been of the folksy type, going to the local library, being received by the chamber of commerce, watching country dancing performed by children from a local dancing school.

During my most recent visit to Perth, a shopping mall held a British Week where they served English tea, hot cross buns, and Bulmer's cider from a wheeled barrow with a Union Jack canopy. Visitors were entertained by Morris dancers, Irish jigs and Scottish pipers. I made recordings for advertising spots on local radio stations, inviting people along to the mall, where I was billed as 'our very special guest'. I picked raffle tickets and handed out prizes ranging from heraldic shields and a stuffed corgi to overseas telephone call tokens and a trip to England. The staff of the mall could wear what they liked, as long as the colours were red, white and blue.

Australians must be the most boat-minded people in the world, and one of the managers of the mall and his wife took me out one weekend on their boat. I was seated on the deck, enjoying the view, the sea, and the sunshine when a frogman suddenly surfaced by the side of us and held out a rose to me. Moments like this are the most memorable. Another was the time I was appearing in Melbourne when a little girl ran out of the audience to take off her treasured pop group badge and give it to me.

Down in the cosmopolitan south-coast city of Adelaide, I was amazed at the number of people who spoke to me about 'home', meaning England. I was also astonished by the number of immigrants from places like Hungary and Eastern Europe who could speak hardly any English but knew all about the Queen.

It was at the Adelaide International Hilton that I encountered the diminutive, doll-like, and extremely pretty Britt Ekland. She ran up to me in the lobby, grabbed my hand and said to a woman with her, 'I want my photograph with Jeannette.' I'd never met Britt at that time, and I still haven't really. Her friend snapped a couple of photographs, and Britt ran off.

Once, when I was making one of my television appearances in Australia, a practical joker called the local police to inform them that the Queen was in town. When I came out of the studio, I found a motorcade waiting for me, complete with outriders. Mistaken identity is one thing, but I think this was going too far.

Mind, I ran into a bit of confusion myself when I arrived at Melbourne Airport. I got off the plane and walked down the steps towards a milling crowd and a group of newspaper photographers. I was wondering why so many people were there when a photographer pushed himself to the front and said, 'Hello, Jeannette, do you remember me?'

'Yes, Tom, I do,' I said. 'But I feel so jaded, would you give me time to freshen up before you take any pictures?'

Tom chuckled and said, 'Don't worry, Jeannette, it's not you we've come to see but Prince Philip. He's been visiting an agricultural show, and is just leaving.'

Boy, was my face red!

And it didn't get any better for me when I went through customs. The officers there laughed and joked with me, which was fine, until I tried to make a joke. 'I won't do a Stonehouse,' I said, and they looked at me in stony silence. I must have touched a raw nerve by mentioning our cabinet minister who hid in Australia after faking his disappearance because my crack was, as Paul Hogan would say, about as popular as a rattlesnake in a lucky dip.

This little hiccup apart, my relations with Australians have been very friendly. I've always received a warm reception and good press coverage there.

A country much closer to home has taken me to its heart, although I think it would take a Sherlock Holmes to fathom the incongruous love affair between the Germans and our royal family.

When my 'second career' was just getting off the ground, the many German mass circulation colour magazines carried a series of articles and off beat photographs of me which ensured I became a public figure there. Now a major proportion of my work is in Germany.

My German television career started with a bang when I was fitted out with a specially made and highly recognisable copy of part of the Queen's wardrobe, which included a large hat and leather gloves. I flew over to Stuttgart, changed into my outfit in one of the plane's lavatories, and prepared to walk down the steps to face a battery of waiting photographers. One of the stewardesses carried my bag containing the discarded clothes, and I managed quite a stately entrance on to German soil.

But serenity was out when we started filming for a variety show, a process which was to take up all of one week. I was in a number of sequences, walking around talking to people, the usual sort of thing. Then I had to walk into a room where I met a rubber-faced comedian who was the star of the show. In character as the Queen, I was supposed to be ready to start my speech.

I sat at a table with about four other people, but every time I opened my mouth, one of the others started to talk. This went on for quite a time, as the scene was shot first from this angle, then from somewhere else. It was still continuing more than two hours later, and I was feeling very, very faint. I had to keep the leather gloves on all the time, and I could feel the constriction starting to have an effect on me.

'Is there a possibility of my having a cup of tea?' I asked.

This resulted in peels of laughter and jokes about 'You English and your tea.' The director ordered, 'Let's get on with it,' and I continued opening my mouth and trying to talk which was all, apparently, I was required to do until suddenly everything went black and I slithered under the table in a dead faint.

When I came to one of the show's writers was leaning over me saying, 'Jeannette, you're in Germany. Come on, now. How do you feel?' His voice sounded very strange and distant but the message was clear: shake to and get back to work. I did, of course, but in the years I've spent in the business since then, I've developed the necessary nerve to call a halt and demand tea or coffee and a few minutes' break when I feel I must rest.

I ended up on the floor again when I made a personal appearance at a vast and magnificent restaurant in Karlsruhe. I changed into my costume at a beautiful baroque-style home, and was led into the celebration evening as a fanfare of trumpets sounded. I sat down at a beautiful table to eat and drink, an operation which was interrupted by the people who were lining up to shake my hand. Then, at the appointed time, I walked over to a microphone to give my prepared speech.

But the burgomaster of the town, one of the star guests, had different plans for me. He strode up to me and, without saying a word, scooped me into his arms and took me off round the room in a whirlwind polka. The polka went faster and faster, and so did we, until I slid right out of the burgomaster's arms, skidded across the floor, and landed up in a most undignified position.

Somebody held out their hand to me and, with all the poise I could muster, I walked slowly back over to the burgomaster and shook his hand. Then I went back to the microphone to deliver my speech. When I had finished, I was given a round of tumultuous applause, but made a mental note to avoid polkas in future.

What the guests thought of my skidding performance I'm not sure, but the German sense of humour is an abiding mystery to me. It is perhaps best demonstrated by the scenario of a comedy show which I appeared in. I played a patient, and a well-known comedian was a psychiatrist. He asked me questions like, 'What is your sister's name?' The answer was, 'Margaret.' 'How is your mother?' 'How old is she?' The replies and answers were those which the Queen would truthfully have given about her family. In the end the 'psychiatrist' thinks he is talking to the real Queen of England and becomes so confused that men in white coats arrive to take him away in a strait jacket.

At the end of the sketch I spoke direct to the audience and blew my cover. I apologised if anybody had been misled, and confessed I was not Queen Elizabeth but an ordinary English housewife. Nevertheless, they still mobbed my car when I left the studios, and those who perhaps were still doubtful about my real identity were confused further by the impressive escort of motorcycle outriders which accompanied my car to the airport.

Definitely and dramatically fooled by my appearance was a gentleman known simply as Herr Fischer who has built up a considerable reputation in Germany by training amateur singers into choirs and conducting them in concerts. He was working with a choir when a call came through to say that the Queen was fogbound at the local airport, and had asked if she could come and see a rehearsal. Herr Fischer was ecstatic, told his choir, and drilled them for their impromptu 'royal' engagement.

I was driven in a Rolls-Royce into a huge auditorium in Stuttgart where he was preparing the choir for a concert scheduled for later that day. We swept in, surrounded by a motorcycle escort, and stopped alongside Herr Fischer. He was smiling, and had clearly fallen for the deception. I spoke to him through the open window of the car. I said I had been very busy but was honoured to be there that day, and to be able to meet him.

The orchestra played, the choir sang, and I stepped out of the car to dance a waltz with the chauffeur – and still Herr Fischer did not rumble what was going on. Then the chauffeur peeled off his moustache to reveal one of Germany's best known television faces, that of the compère of '*Verstehen Sie Spatz*?' which means 'Do You Understand Fun?' and is the unwieldy Teutonic translation of 'Candid Camera'. The freeze-frame at the end of this particular piece of film showed exactly how embarrassed Herr Fischer felt at being 'had'.

Equally fooled by the illusion, but delighted with it, was a little girl in a wheelchair at Hamburg Airport. I had just flown in for an appearance on a television show, and had been given an escort of 'security guards' who were really extras dressed up for the occasion. They walked with me across the concourse, people were shouting and waving at me, and I was about to get into a waiting car when a lady came up to me and said in broken English, 'You are so sweet. You are so lovely. We are proud to have the Queen of England here. My daughter has never met the Queen, and she is so happy. Could she have a photograph with you, please?' I said she certainly could, and I stood by the little girl in her wheelchair while the photograph was taken. The girl's delighted expression told me how much the Queen meant to her.

A boy who dreamed of meeting the Queen was brought on to a television chat show in Hamburg to meet me. Torstan Kroop had so wanted to meet Her Majesty that he had written to ask for an invitation to a garden party at Buckingham Palace, and had received one. But the party was so vast, and the crowds so dense, that he had not been able to get near the Queen, so the German chat show host thought he would provide him with an introduction to the next best thing, and young Torstan was delighted.

There was a bit of a surprise waiting for me when I went over to appear on a television spectacular staged by Rudi Karel, a Dutchman living in Germany. He specialises in featuring unusual artists during his variety shows, and he thought it would be a novel idea to get the 'Queen of England' to come on to the show and knight him.

It was set up very well. Trumpeters played me in, the National Anthem was struck up by the orchestra, and a group of dignitaries lined up to greet me. The audience were fooled and all stood up – it was just like 'Candid Camera'.

I walked in wearing a satin turquoise outfit, shook Rudi by the hand, and an official standing next to him handed me an enormous sword which looked incredibly heavy but was in fact made of plastic. I asked Rudi to kneel down, then pretended that the sword was much too heavy for me to lift. I made a big show of struggling to raise it in the air, staggered with it raised high, and toppled back into a chair behind me. All this was part of the script, and I had rehearsed it carefully. What they had not told me was that the chair was fitted with a swivel so that when I landed in it the back gave way, and I fell backwards with my legs in the air. The audience roared with laughter, but the most surprised person in that studio was me. The sword had flown from my hand and broken.

Rudi came to help me up as I was feeling quite shaken but I recovered sufficiently to make a dignified exit from the studio. This show was screened all over German-speaking Western Europe and did a lot to put my name on the map there. It is now considered a classic of its kind.

Another Queen-seeker turned out to be Inge Meysel, a German character actress in the Bette Davis mould. She was invited into a Hamburg television studio ostensibly for an interview which turned out to be a surprise 75th birthday party with many of her old co-stars in attendance. The interviewer said, 'You've never been to London but you've always wanted to see the Queen, haven't you?'

'Oh, yes, it's been a dream for years.'

At that moment, a fanfare of trumpets followed by the opening bars of 'Land of Hope and Glory' heralded my arrival. Curtains parted behind Inge, revealing me standing in a 'royal box'. I read out a speech in German, saying how I would like Elke to come over to London.

In Cologne, I appeared in a television documentary called 'The Historical Bed', which was about a castle many hundreds of years old which had been turned into a hotel. The lobby contained a list of European royalty who had stayed there down the centuries, ending up with our own Queen and Prince Philip. They had used the same room. In fact, they had used the same bed, which was still there. Actors and actresses were brought in to play the rôles of former royalty, and I was imported to play the Queen. For my sequence I put on a nightdress and a dressing gown and sat up in the bed, reading a book. A man's voice off screen said something like, 'Well, darling, what would you like to drink?' and I replied, 'A nice cup of tea, of course.'

German industry has also used my presence to promote its products. I've been to trade fairs in Stuttgart and Hanover, and to Frankfurt to attract attention for an association of shoe traders. I wanted to take some shoes home from this latter event but my request produced a Cinderella-like episode for I take size 40 shoes in the continental measurement which is unusually small for Germany. After quite a search, they managed to produce a nice white pair for me.

I've been the resident celebrity at Worms, during the traditional annual drinkers' festival known as the Bierfast, and had the pleasure of serving a stein of beer from the pump.

A natural for me has been the travelling exhibition 'Kronen aus Allerwelt', which translates as something like 'Crowns from Around the World'. This is a rich German's private collection of replicas of crown jewels of many of the world's royal families. He doesn't like to keep them hidden away in a museum, preferring that his collection should be out on display where people can see it, so he takes it to various towns around Germany. It includes, of course, the British Crown of State, and I have worn that to open his exhibitions on several occasions.

Because I found myself going to Germany so much, I decided to start taking private German lessons, and to make a habit of reading German for at least an hour a day. It's a language I have taken to and, for example, when I went to the beautiful spa town of Baden Baden to appear at a shopping mall, it was so much fun to be able to walk around talking to spectators.

I have handed out prizes and long service medals at company annual general meetings, and appeared in German magazine advertisements for products like milk chocolate and a liqueur which is recommended as a fiery addition to a cup of tea. For the liqueur promotion, I was photographed sipping a cup of tea and surrounded by a crowd of men in bowler hats. It was a very effective campaign, and it increased sales.

I got carried away in a promotional video made in Germany for F.U.S. Jeans. This film opens with a shot from behind a lady wearing jeans, with her top half adorned with queenly regalia, complete with a little crown. The lady turns round and, of course, it's me. A Tarzan-type man then steps into shot, picks me up and walks off with me.

When that film was made, I turned up at the studio in my full regalia but someone told me, 'We only need the top because we're going to put you into jeans.'

'What are you going to do?' I asked.

'Cut the dress in half, of course,' was the reply. So cut it was, and that was the only time I've had to come home with half a dress.

The idea of calling me in was sparked off because F.U.S. jeans had just incorporated a new logo, the Union Jack. The resultant video was screened on a stand at a Cologne trading fair and I was there too, sitting by the monitor to attract buyers to the F.U.S. exhibit. A section of the video was shown on television in Britain, in Clive James's 'Clive James on TV', a hilarious look at the viewing tastes of other nations.

I received the ultimate in advertising accolades when I went to Munich to film a commercial for McDonalds, the hamburger chain. I was driven up to the restaurant in a limousine, which attracted a lot of attention. A lady approached as we were setting up our equipment to present me with a red rose, and a young girl ran over from a nearby shop to curtsey to me. In the advertising film I am shown from behind, walking up to the counter. The girl assistant looks astounded to see me, then the next shot from behind her shows my face. I say, 'Big Mac, *bitte*,' am given a hamburger, and take a large bite.

An enterprising young hairdresser called Martin Jacobson invited me to Berlin for the fifth anniversary party of his 'Hair Power' salon. That was great fun, but the required touristic delight of a trip through Checkpoint Charlie, the strictly controlled entrance to East Berlin, terrified me.

My visit to West Berlin had received a lot of local publicity, but I was under the impression that the people of East Berlin had no access to newspapers from the West. However, when I was passing through the series of security doors on the checkpoint, the bored young border guards in their uniforms knew all about me. I heard them talking in German about the Queen, and they produced a West Berlin newspaper with headlines about my visit.

Martin Jacobson, as a West Berliner, had to go through a different way, and I met him on the other side to have a drive around. I was scared stiff the whole time.

The East Berliners have an interesting currency racket. When tourists pass through from the West, they are obliged to buy five marks of local currency. On the return trip, the Eastern authorities confiscate the money, saying it is illegal to export currency. But when I came back through, the soldiers were so busy talking to me in the smattering of English at their command that they forgot the money. So I have a five-mark East German coin as a souvenir.

A couple of months later, I got a telephone call from Martin to say that if I returned to Berlin a television company would make a documentary on his salon. So I headed back, and appeared in the film along with the other well-known faces he could muster. The opening shot of the documentary showed me being driven up to my hotel on the back of a motorbike, which was a great attention grabber.

When the filming was taking place in the salon, the Queen happened to be on an official visit to Berlin. I borrowed a dark wig from Martin's stock and slipped out to stand in the crowd to take a look at Her Majesty as she stood on a podium to deliver a speech.

Germans have mostly been very courteous and friendly to me wherever I have appeared. There is, however, an exception which I will always remember, and which made me wonder how much of the old Nazi regime still lives.

I was leaving through Frankfurt Airport, and came to the security gate carrying a handbag, a little carryall, and a plastic bag containing three hats which were part of my professional wardrobe. I had not packed them because I didn't want them to be crushed.

A huge, powerfully built woman in a security uniform told me I could only take my handbag and one of the bags. The bag of hats was light as a feather which I told her. 'If you don't mind, I won't put the carrier bag into the other bag or the carryall into the bag of hats,' I said.

Anyone else would have turned a blind eye but this authoritarian bully said, 'You are permitted one. Queen or no Queen. One.' Then she turned her head to one side and pretended to spit, a look of pure venom in her eyes.

I went immediately back to the concourse and asked for the controller of the airport. He turned up, a very friendly man, and asked how he could help. I said, 'I've just come from a television show in Germany, and I've got this small bag here with three hats in it. I've also got a carryall.'

'That will be all right.'

'But what about that officer? She won't let me through.'

'Oh, I'll have a word with her,' he said, and went off. He had a word with her and came back looking ashamed. 'She says that if you go through with those, she'll stop work and bring the airport to a standstill. I'm really very sorry, but I can't do anything.'

'Are you absolutely sure?' I said amazed. 'The bag weighs hardly anything, and look at the large bags other people are taking through.' He just shrugged helplessly and I saw red. 'All right, I'll show you what I'm going to do,' I said.

I put the plastic bag with the three hats in it on the floor and jumped up and down on it. Then I stormed through the security gate, glaring at the woman but saying not a word. She went scarlet. I looked ahead of me and saw two soldiers with machine guns standing by the curtain over the gangway leading to the plane. I glared at them, they stood their guns down and stepped aside, and I swept past.

It was a vastly different story when I was leaving Hamburg Airport later that same year. A woman came over to me from the check-in desk and said, 'I'd like your autograph and your picture.' Then somebody else wanted one. I gave them both signed photographs, marked 'To all the staff at Hamburg Airport.' When I next arrived to pass through the same airport on my way to an engagement they were all over me, from the passport control onwards.

It's nice to be remembered like that.

Italy has fascinated me since I was a young girl, and I'm always delighted to be asked to go there. I gained a lot of recognition from the whisky advertisements many years ago, and the Italians seem as keen on our royals as the Germans. I appeared in several clips of a humourous television chat show called '*Cipria*,' in which I was interviewed on matters royal by a Signora Enzo Tortora, a truly charming man who has since been arrested, suspected of being a member of the Camorra, the Neapolitan version of the Mafia.

In Milan, I guested in a television show called 'Drive-In', with a comedy actor who played Prince Charles as a very naughty boy whom I was obliged to smack.

I went to Rome to appear in a television film called 'The Dream', and decided to go off on a shopping expedition. I was just enjoying a stroll down Rome's equivalent of Oxford Street when a woman came out of the shop and said in Italian, 'She's the Queen.' In no time at all, a crowd had gathered, and everybody seemed to be jabbering away at me. I still don't speak Italian, and it became rather frightening.

Luckily a lady turned up who spoke English and I said to her, 'I am very scared, and I want to get back to my hotel. Will you help me get a taxi?'

'I'll get you a taxi, of course, but could I have a photograph with you?' So I posed for the photograph, the taxi arrived, and I went back to the hotel, all ideas of a shopping expedition abandoned.

The day I was headed for Linz, Austria, to open a wonderful new shopping mall just happened to coincide with a strike by air traffic controllers at London Airport so I telephoned the developers in Linz to tell them I could not get there. Their response was, 'But you've got to come! We've advertised and we have thousands of people who are coming just to see you.' They laid on a private jet to fly me from Luton to Austria. At Linz Airport, a magnificent open top vintage car, dating from the early 1900s, was waiting for me, driven by the Count whose family owned and had preserved the car. He was dressed up in the most beautiful Tyrolean outfit, complete with feathered hat and shining buttons.

The Count escorted me to the car and drove me to his family's castle where I spent the night in truly regal splendour. Next morning, I was driven with a motorcycle escort into Linz, along roads jam-packed with people waving flags and cheering. At the shopping mall I was directed up a rickety flight of stairs, which felt as if they were made of cardboard, to sit on a high seat. Then the children were invited to come upstairs to meet me, and our combined weight and movement started swaying the whole structure. I thought it was going to fall over. It didn't, but I was relieved to get back down to earth, to walk around chatting to the visitors and practise my German.

I was a conspicuous V.I.P., and the Austrians clearly decided to take no chances. Two soldiers with rifles and fixed bayonets were placed outside my hotel door that night. When I peeked out in the morning, they were still standing there.

An entirely different type of engagement awaited me in Vienna where I recorded a television show. This was filmed shortly after Michael Fagin had been discovered in the Queen's bedroom at Buckingham Palace, and my scene called for me to sit under a quilt while the classic busker Dave Kay sang, 'Once I Had A Secret Love'.

At the other end of Europe, I got a grandstand view of the Queen and Prince Philip as they drove past my hotel in Helsinki, Finland. I knew exactly how the Queen felt because the day before I had covered the same route at the request of the local authorities who had wanted to get their timings and protocol carefully regulated. I had besides been invited by a local magazine to be photographed in the various locations the Queen was to visit, and was delighted to take the time to assist the Queen's hosts as I did so.

I went to Oslo, Norway, to be the surprise guest at the first birthday party of a British-owned disco, and I posed for a calendar poster produced by a language school in Stockholm, Sweden. For the poster, I wore a crown and the cloak of the Order of the Garter, and the caption below read, 'My children speak perfect English. What about yours?'

I flew to Switzerland to be the surprise guest at a birthday party, and at a gala given by *Glucks Post* magazine of Zurich, I made a speech from a mock throne. In a very funny moment at the gala, a muscular young man dressed in a loincloth swung in on a rope, grabbed me, regalia and all, and disappeared with me. Later, I returned to Zurich to attract publicity as a guest at a party given by the jeweller, Harry Hoffman, but my biggest splash in that city came with a television commercial for Migros Restaurants, a chain which specialises in fish and chips.

I was filmed with a whole bunch of lookalikes, including the Pope, Joan Collins, and Charles and Diana. I tucked into a plate of fish and chips, and when Charles took some of my chips I smacked his hand. The British Ambassador over there complained and the story got into the local papers. The ever-resourceful owner of Migros used this incident to set up a second commercial. It was the same as the first, except that in this one I was shown in the restaurant reading a newspaper with the headline 'Protest against British Queen eating in Migros'. What the ambassador thought of this I don't know, but you could say the restaurant made a meal of his complaint!

CHAPTER NINE

Perfecting the Art

My 'second career' had hardly begun when I realised that just to have a face resembling the Queen's was not enough. I had to do more than look the part; I had to work on the other aspects of my presentation and change myself from a raw royal lookalike to someone who could give a total impression of the Queen. I had to get the details right, and to achieve that I have studied everything about the Queen: her voice, her mannerisms, her walk, her clothes.

The voice was perhaps the easiest for me to emulate. One thing that is marvellous about the Queen is that, unlike so many of the other members of the upper class, she has what I call a mid-cultured accent. She used to have a very high-pitched girlish voice, with oversensitive high tones, and I can remember newspapers urging that she should lower it because it grated rather. I understand that she had a voice coach to rectify this. She now has a well-modulated voice with an educated accent, but not too educated. She has the kind of voice which makes people immediately attentive. It is not a very difficult accent to imitate as long as I remember to speak that little bit slower, to round off my a's and o's, and to enunciate the ends of words, particularly those finishing with t's and d's. She has a very clear, distinctive voice in which every word hits home.

I've taped her voice many times, playing it back and mimicking it slavishly. The Queen's annual Christmas message to the Commonwealth has been obligatory listening for me for many, many years. I record it, listen to it; record my own version of it, listen to it; record myself again, adjusting my tone where necessary, honing and refining and perfecting as I go. I used to have people abroad who wanted to book me asking for tapes of my speaking voice, and I'd prepared these 'in character'. If I get a speech sent to me in advance for an engagement, I deliver it over again and again into a tape recorder until I am happy with it.

Comments from other people about how I sound have been invaluable. On my first visit to Australia, a lady pointed out to me that I said Australia in the conventional way. She said, 'You were perfect except for one thing: the Queen always says "Orstraulia".' And of course she does. I assimilated this and now I say a very good 'Orstraulia'.

My diligence has paid off, I'm glad to say. My client list is proof of that. I'm glad to give good value, believing that if people are willing to pay me considerable fees to appear at their functions they deserve more than just a familiar face. I think I have captured the Queen's voice as precisely as anyone can, and can slip into it at the drop of a hat when a job of work demands it.

Perhaps my lifelong love of acting helped me to tackle the rôle of the Queen for now I feel I am very much an actress who looks like the Queen and can bring her character to life. It's strange that I always wanted to be an actress, and ended up playing this one highly specialised rôle.

A man who contributed much to my achievement was a certain Jimmy Jacobs who called himself an act-doctor. I knew that if I were to operate as a professional, I would need advice and training. I happened to be flicking through the pages of *The Stage* and spotted Jimmy's advertisement which offered help with voice acting, and general presentation. I found out later that he was a very highly respected comedian who had been associated in his early life with people like Issy Bonn and Vic Oliver. I learned a lot from Jimmy about acquiring confidence in my performance in front of an audience. He told me, 'Hold your head up, speak to them, and include them in your script. That way they will be part of it and enjoy it, and you will always have the audience with you.'

He wrote me some one-liners which I could use in my speech, and advised me to use the same words that the Queen uses as then I would have a much better chance of sounding like her. He was also great in helping me to master the Queen's intonations. He was a wise and very lovely man. I saw him three times, and was shocked to hear that he had died just two days after our last session. He managed to give me much to build on, and I will always remember him with gratitude.

Whenever I can, I watch the Queen on television and over the years I have videoed her on royal tours, doing walkabouts, and giving speeches. I have watched them time and time again to learn her walk and her mannerisms. I also have videos of myself doing personal appearances, and I watch these to see what I can do to improve my presentation. I am still refining and improving my performance.

When I was first asked to make personal appearances, I assumed that anything nice I had to wear would be fine. Dressing well in good clothes is of vital importance, certainly, but I started to realise that I would need to invest in a specialised wardrobe. As the various assignments came in for television and private jobs, I started spending a considerable amount on queenly evening dresses, afternoon dresses, and two-piece suits, even the full regalia, for I could not rely on people who booked me to supply what I needed to enhance my rôle. I've also accumulated a collection of accessories, including replicas of jewels from the royal collection, especially the pearls and drop-earrings the Queen loves. I even have a crown, copied from the one that appears on our postage stamps. An added bonus of my Equity membership has been the fitting fees I've been able to claim for supplying my own outfit.

The hairstyle has never been a problem for me. I've always worn my hair in an off the face style, probably as long as the Queen herself.

Some people have suggested I should broaden my repertoire. I was once offered the chance of making a record, and given a recording audition at which apparently, I was totally flat. The promoter said my voice might be all right for narrating fairy tales which sounded suspiciously like, 'Don't call me, I'll call you.'

When I was approached about developing a song and dance act, my thoughts raced back to my few days at the Intimate Theatre and I declined. I don't think that sort of thing is for me. I'm better off staying with what I do well.

I felt honoured to be asked by the Walt Disney company to take part in a video of greetings from around the world wishing Donald Duck a happy fiftieth birthday. I said how much pleasure I'd got from Donald Duck over the years, how my children and grandchildren had all grown up loving him, and were firm fans. Any time Donald came to London, I concluded, he was most welcome to come and see me.

When I made a Christmas video for the staff of MFI at Reading, I co-starred with an employee dressed up as Father Christmas. I walked around congratulating the company's salesmen on their achievements, and talked about my hopes for the future. The Managing Director of the company was in America at the time of filming, and they planned to screen the video for him at the firm's Christmas party and tell him he had missed a visit from the Queen.

I sat at a desk to record a video message for *Retailing World*, a trade magazine, which was shown on a special evening when managers and manageresses of retail shops all over the country were invited. My speech was tailored to the audience, and dwelt on inflation and food prices.

The Marie Antoinette Suite at The Ritz was the setting for a scene incorporated into a Brooke Bond tea promotion video which was used all over the Middle East. I sat at a table with directors of the company discussing English tea in general, and Brooke Bond tea in particular. The directors really loved it, and I understood they all asked for personal copies of the video.

The Middle East was also the target for a Softee Tissue promotional video which had me arriving by car at a beautiful country house near Beaconsfield, walking in, sneezing, and asking for a tissue.

For many years, Jerry Hall, the world's top model, and I have been co-stars of a series of Mexican television commercials advertising jeans. The makers were prompted to use me because of the brand name of their product, Britannia Jeans.

When the first commercial was filmed, we could not start work until ten thirty at night because the producers had rented a theatre as our set and we had to wait for the audience to go home. We worked through the night, which was exhausting, but the end product was worth all the effort. In the film, I walked into the theatre where Jerry and a bunch of other models, all wearing Britannia Jeans, were lined up for my inspection at the bottom of a breathtaking, sweeping staircase. I look at the jeans and stand back in theatrical amazement.

Another of my commercials for this company featured Jerry dancing on stage wearing a beautiful dress, which she raised to reveal a pair of Britannia Jeans. In a third version, I walk through a hall and looked out of a window to see young people dancing in the street wearing, yes, you guessed it, Britannia Jeans! I say, 'Oh, that's lovely, now I know the way out.' Then I step out through clouds of fog, manufactured to reproduce the British climate, I presume, to where the youngsters are disco dancing.

I found Jerry a refreshingly open and friendly girl who would sit around and talk about Mick Jagger just as any woman might discuss her man.

Apart from the commercials on television, the jeans manufacturers also used this advertising theme in leaflets and bookmatches which contained photographs of me with Beefeaters and the strikingly elegant Jerry Hall.

I understand that the British Ambassador in Mexico complained about the television advertisements, and the producer told him to go to hell.

I found out the impact the commercials had on Mexican viewers when my husband, Ken, and I happened to drive across into Tijuana from California during an American holiday. We went to a market place where Ken started haggling with a shopkeeper selling leather bags. People were stopping to look at me, and in no time we had quite a crowd gathered round. Then they started following us as we made our way through the market, which brought more people over to gape and ask for autographs. In the end we had to get back in the car and head for the border.

An invitation to a London reception brought me a trip to Brazil and an appearance in what I consider one of my most amusing television commercials. The reception was the prelude to a lunch for the worldwide representatives of the J. Walter Thompson advertising agency, held at their Mayfair offices. I was recruited to stand at the door dressed very like the Queen in a two-piece suit and hat, and to greet the people arriving with a handshake and perhaps a few words. It was going very smoothly until a Frenchman came in and thought that I really was the Queen. He started chatting away to me in French, a language which I don't understand but which I know the Queen speaks very well. I wanted to escape him but I didn't want to disillusion the poor fellow so I developed a diplomatic coughing fit and managed to slip away.

I went over to the public relations girl who was looking after me, told her what had happened and asked, 'What am I going to do?' She said, 'You'd better keep away from him.' I tried to, hiding myself behind little groups of people while the poor man ranged the room looking for me.

I was trying hard to conceal myself in a corner of the room when a man walked over to me and said, 'I want you in my commercial.'

'Do you?' I said, still looking round nervously for the Frenchman. 'What are you advertising?'

'English tea biscuits.'

The man, it transpired, was Ivan Pinto from São Paulo, Brazil, and the boss of a company which makes Petybon biscuits. He told me, 'It's been driving me crazy, trying to think of an idea for a commercial. I want you.'

'Well,' I said, 'that's fine. If it can be arranged, by all means.' Then I went back to hiding from the questing Frenchman.

A couple of months later, I flew out to Brazil to make Mr Pinto's commercial. In it I sit, dressed in queenly fashion, in an ornate room. Close beside me is a table with a packet of the tea biscuits on it. A butler comes in, pours a cup of tea and hands it to me. When I ask for a biscuit, he passes me the packet. I take the biscuit, turn to the camera and say, 'I am not the genuine Queen, but this is a genuine Petybon biscuit.'

The commercial was made in both English and Portuguese, and was aimed at creating a market for English tea biscuits in the Brazilian market. It won awards all over the world.

It was a great success, but it could have been a disaster. When we were actually preparing for the filming in the studio, a curtain near me went up in flames. I watched, mesmerised, then called out, 'There's a fire over there.' People started dashing about all over the place, in a typical Latin panic. Nothing was being done about the fire, but they were flying this way and that. Finally, the fire was put out without my moving from my chair.

Mr Pinto came up to me and said admiringly, 'You know, madam, you are so-o British.' He didn't know I had remained immobile for one reason only – I was frozen with fear.

I went to New York to make a commercial for The Red Lobster chain of restaurants. My companions were all lookalikes from history and the present day. A Henry VIII, a George IV, a Henry Kissinger, myself as Elizabeth II (what a surprise!), and many more. We were all given one-liners to deliver. In my scene, I hold a lobster in my hand and say to Henry VIII, 'I do like a man with good legs.'

The filming took a long time, and I got very hungry waiting around. There was a buffet of bread, cheese and pickles available for the actors, but I could not resist the lobsters we had used in the filming. They were the biggest and fleshiest I had ever seen. I started pulling the flesh off and nibbling away. I love lobsters. Who doesn't?

What I didn't realise was that the same lobsters had been there as props during several days of filming. Unlike the beautiful fresh lobsters the restaurant chain served, these creatures were quite elderly. When I got back to the hotel that night, I was very ill with food poisoning and spent most of my time in the bathroom. I had recovered by the next day but I've always wondered: if the poisoning had proved fatal, would it have been regicide?

Wherever I go in the world, I always seem to find my own face looking back at me from magazine displays in shops and airport bookstalls – like the time I was pictured on the cover of the German magazine, *Stern*, sitting on a tandem while a chauffeur pumped up the rear tyre, or on the cover of a home-grown magazine, *Catch*, where I was depicted reading a copy of the journal over the caption, 'The best people read *Catch*.'

I got the David Bailey treatment with a group of face-painted models when we were photographed for a *Vanity Fair* spread. I modelled with crown, orb, and sceptre when an American company put replicas of the British crown jewels on display near Disneyland, California, and the resultant photographs went round the world. When my old friend, Arthur Steel, of the *Sun*, wanted to set up a photograph around the time of the Prince Andrew–Koo Stark stories, he got me to pose, looking suitably shocked, while I held up a newspaper headlining the romance.

Work with pop singers added a dimension to my career which I would never have envisaged a few years ago.

My first venture called for me to be photographed looking very harassed and jaded, wearing a dressing-gown and standing in a rundown kitchen. It was used to illustrate a booklet issued with the LP 'Quadrophenia,' recorded by The Who. I later appeared in a more formal blue dress and pearls and, for some reason, sipping a cup of tea, on the cover of a record by The Average White Band. And when Captain Sensible wanted two women being lowered into lifeboats from a liner for his LP cover, he chose a Margaret Thatcher lookalike and myself.

Personal appearances in this area of British showbusiness got under way for me at the Café Royal when I presented a silver disc to the pop group Queen, so they had 'the Queen' presenting an award to Queen.

When the American singer, Alice Cooper, completed a British tour with a Wembley show, I was called in to attend an after event party and present him with a gold disc award for sales of a record in Australia. I turned up in my full regalia, complete with tiara, and when I was presented to Alice Cooper he fell on one knee with his head bowed. He had not been told I would be there, and was taken in completely.

The party had wall to wall celebrities. I met Richard Chamberlain, David Essex, Lynsey de Paul, and many others. Peter Sellers was particularly charming.

'Jeannette, you've brought something new to the industry,' he told me. He also promised, 'I'll see what I can do for you.' It was not long after this that I got an invitation to appear on television with his old friend, Spike Milligan, but I'll never know if Peter engineered this.

I was the surprise guest in the 'royal box' at an Earls Court concert by Status Quo where I was confronted by a crowd of thousands of screaming youngsters. The din was beyond belief, and really scared me.

I opened a concert for Gary Glitter and his Glitter Band, and was staggered at the spectacle of all the fans dressed in glittering clothes and waving glittering banners which I think were made of tin foil.

The audience were making so much noise that no one could have heard a word I said when I went to an open air auditorium to present a silver disc to the group Heavy Metal. We got mobbed, and the car was stopped by the crowd. That, too, was very frightening.

A group with the improbable name of The Screamers booked me, along with actors Denis Waterman and Robert Powell, for an album promotion. I went to the appointed venue, a room in a West End hotel, where I spotted a coffin laid out on stage.

I was told, 'We want you to walk over to the coffin, climb into it, and lie down. Then The Screamers will scream.'

'You can't ask me to do that,' I said firmly.

'We can,' came the reply. 'That's why we've got you here today.'

'In that case,' I said, 'I'll leave now.'

The organiser tried to insist, on the basis that they were paying for my work that day. I said I would stand by the coffin if somebody else wanted to get in it, but that was all. It ended up with my being introduced from the front of the audience as a 'very special person here today' and being led over to look at someone dressed as Dracula who was lying in the coffin.

A lighter prospect was offered by The Piranhas group and a video they were producing to publicise a new record. The location was outside the old labour exchange at Richmond, and I stood, dressed in regalia and crown, in line with the group who were all dressed as tramps. Their new record started playing, and we all shuffled along to the music. Then another of the Piranhas stepped out of the door of the old labour exchange building, holding aloft a great big stick with a rooster on top and calling out 'Next!' The first person in our line walked in, and the rest of us continued shuffling to the beat. And so it went on.

A man who had spotted us as he walked into the new labour exchange came out and walked across to us. He looked along our line in a puzzled way then asked me, 'You waiting for your money, missus?' The members of the group looked at me, not sure what to make of this development.

'Well, yes, actually I am,' I said. 'In fact, we all are.'

The man eyed me quizzically and said, 'Do you really need the money?'

'Oh, yes, I really do. I haven't got much to live on, and I've got a family to support. I've even got grandchildren.'

'Then I don't know what you're standing here for, missus, 'cos that's where you gotta go.' And he pointed up the road to the new labour exchange. 'This is the *old* building,' he said, then shook his head wonderingly and turned away up the road.

The group fell all over the place, laughing. I did, too, though I hadn't dared to laugh while the man was talking to me. The director told us to take a rest and try the sequence again. Apparently he had the whole conversation on film and said it would look great on 'It'll Be All Right on the Night'.

We started up again. The Piranha with the rooster on a stick came out, and the next person in our line went in. We were all shuffling again, when I could hardly believe it – our friend came strolling back. He held out some money in his hand and said to me, 'Look, you see how much money I've got?'

'It's not very much, is it?'

'No, it isn't. Can't you do anything about it?'

'Well, I'll try. But you know these fellow here' – and I pointed to The Piranhas – 'they need help, too.'

'Oh,' he said, 'is that why you're here?'

'Yes, actually, it is.'

He was still standing there, examining us, so I said, 'Look, why don't you give me a call at Buckingham Palace and we'll see what we can do for you.'

'Oh, thank you very much, missus,' he said, and tipped his cap. 'Have you got the number?'

'No, I'm sorry, you'll have to look in Yellow Pages.'

With that, he turned and walked off leaving us to film undisturbed.

The cameras were running all the time he was speaking to me. Every single, crazy moment was captured. What they did with that film I don't know, but with our unscheduled extra out of the way, we managed to complete the video. I'm sure it wasn't a patch on the impromptu version.

CHAPTER TEN

The Queen & I

Very soon after I set out on my chosen course of being a professional lookalike of the Queen, I took it upon myself to write to Her Majesty offering a solemn undertaking that I would always avoid doing anything distasteful or disrespectful to royalty. Despite the claims of some more disreputable newspapers to the contrary, I have honoured that pledge. I would not consider doing anything that pokes fun at the Queen. I think Her Majesty is a wonderful woman, and I wouldn't dream of doing anything that might offend her.

The television commercials and magazine advertising I have undertaken, I consider to be good fun and in no way derisory. In fact, all of my work is tastefully handled. I undertake nothing grotesque, rude or indecent, not only out of respect for the Queen but also for my self.

Over the years, I have been offered open cheque books to undertake work more in line with that usually offered to Page Three girls. In fact, the fees could have made me very rich, and I've been called all kinds of fools for turning down these offers but who needs money that badly? What's the good even of vaults full of money if my self-respect is forfeited?

If I even remotely suspect the job on offer, I turn it down. I've spent many years building up my reputation for integrity and I have no intention of throwing it away now. People know that I have certain standards, and that is one of the reasons I am still in demand.

Like most things, the dubious offers started on a small scale. I can remember quite a while ago being asked to drive around in a Rolls-Royce handing out leaflets advertising squatters' rights. The people who made this offer were waiting to speak to me outside a hotel, where I had been for an audition. My refusal had nothing to do with whether I support the rights of squatters or not. I was annoyed that they wanted to use me and, indirectly, the Queen, in this way.

An even stranger request came my way during a studio photographic assignment when a young fellow walked swiftly up to me, holding a banner in his hand, and said, 'Can I have a photo taken with you.'

I was about to agree, when I looked at the sign. It read 'Drugs are OK'. 'Oh, no you don't,' I told him, and got away as fast as I could.

A mysterious telephone caller once asked me to go across to Belfast to appear in some kind of rally. I was annoyed at this, and also scared. A request to attend the opening of the trendy Bennett's Restaurant in

Battersea seemed a good idea until I discovered they wanted me to walk in on the arm of Roddy Llewellyn, the well-known former friend of Princess Margaret.

There was a story some while ago about a woman who was sent to Holloway Jail for defying a court order and taking her three dogs through a park. I was furious when the BBC asked me to stand outside the prison with three corgis on leashes to meet the lady when she was released. How stupid I would have looked!

Other people have tried to set me up in situations which would have put me in confrontation with the Queen, like the time I was booked to open the extension of a store in Argyle Street, a main shopping thoroughfare of Glasgow. On the eve of this assignment, I got a telephone call from a reporter on a Glasgow newspaper, who said, 'We've all had a press release telling us you're going to open the shop where you'll be in sight of the Queen who will be in the same street, opening the Glasgow underground. If you want to guard your reputation, you'd better not come up.'

I felt sick. I called my agent, and the response was, 'You'll have to go, or pay compensation for not turning up.' I said there was no question of my going, and I didn't.

A request to appear at a public house in Rochester, Kent, at eleven in the morning got me thinking, for that is a very unusual time for an assignment of this type. My agent asked the publican the reason, and was told that the Queen was to be in Rochester that same day. It seemed that she would not be going to the area of the town where this public house was located, though she might come pretty close. The publican said he and other members of the shopkeepers' association who were being missed by the Queen's visit wanted me there as a substitute in their part of town.

My response was 'Forget it', but somehow the press got wind of it and my agent got a call asking: 'Is it true that Jeannette Charles is going to be in Rochester and in view of the Queen while she is visiting the town?' The publican went on television to explain why he had wanted to hire a 'rival Queen', and later telephoned to say, 'I respect Jeannette as an artist and a person, and I don't want her to think that I wanted to put two fingers up to the Queen.'

I was delighted to be interviewed and photographed for the French magazine *Paris Match* by a charming couple who came over to England. They photographed me at home, in my garden, then the woman said, 'We'd like you to come over to France for a couple of weeks.'

It sounded like a nice idea and so I said: 'What do you want me to do there?'

'We've got a few ideas in mind. We'll take you up the Eiffel Tower, to the Arc de Triomphe, to a few cabarets, perhaps to the red light district of Montmartre.' I had an immediate vision of the girls and their clients waving to me from balconies as I passed down the street.

'Let's get one thing clear,' I said. 'The Queen is a very respectable lady. I'm sorry, but I can't do that sort of thing.'

'We'll put you up in the George Cinque Hotel, and you can practically have an open cheque book. What's it to you if you go down the red light district? The Queen and other royalty, you can't know everywhere they go.'

My answer was still definitely no, and they said, 'Well, you're very silly. You could earn a lot of money. You've had a lot of publicity. Maybe this is the end for you.'

I would rather have ended my career, there and then, than do something which could disgrace the image of the Queen. I showed the visitors the door.

I was even offered a lot of money to attend an orgy on a Thames boat. Just imagine what photographs of that would have done to the Queen's image, never mind mine.

One evening I got a call from a man in San Francisco who said, 'I've just seen you on the "Laugh-In" programme, and I think you're wonderful. Would you consider coming over to open my restaurant?' So I put him in touch with my agent who rang to say, 'You're not going to like this, Jeannette, but they want you to open the restaurant wearing a Merry Widow outfit.'

Naïvely, I said, 'That's rather nice, isn't it?'

'Not exactly. They want you to wear this strapless dress with an uplift bodice so you look like Mae West with a tiara on your head!'

A calendar publisher wanted me to be photographed looking slightly tipsy, my crown askew. If that wasn't bad enough, they wanted me to wear nothing *but* the crown. It's not funny. I don't like even to be asked things like that.

Then there was a photographer who said he had a commission for a businessman's calendar, and wanted to feature me as Miss January. I said, 'I'd love to. What do you want me to wear.'

His answer threw me. 'Oh, fishnet tights, bra, and panties,' he said. 'That type of thing.'

'You're joking,' I said.

'No, we'll pay you a lot of money.'

I delivered a crisp 'No thank you', and put the phone down.

Another caller said, 'Mrs Charles, would you consider – now, take it slowly – would you consider being our centrefold. We'll give you £5,000.'

'Which one are you, *Penthouse* or *Playboy*?' I said wearily.

'I'd rather not say at the moment,' he hedged, 'but would you consider it?'

'You must be joking or insane. A woman like me, at my age?'

'Oh, no,' he said, 'we're not joking. In fact, I think they might go higher. I'll ring you back.'

I sat there, stunned, and he phoned back later to say, 'I'm sure we can go up to £10,000. Would you like to come up and see us.' No, I would not!

I slipped up when I took a five-minute bit part in a film which I thought was a comedy. In fact, it turned out to be a raunchy sex film called 'Confessions of a Superstud'. There was nothing naughty about my scene, but I would never have agreed to appear if I'd known the type of film it really was. I was sickened and ashamed to be so caught out, and I've made sure nothing like this has happened since.

The newspapers launched an attack on me over this, with headlines like 'We are not amused'. I have that in my scrapbook of newspaper tirades for, every once in a while, the press turns hostile towards me. 'Jeannette upsets the Palace', and 'What a cheek she has', were headlines over stories which attacked rôles like the one in the German television documentary 'The Historical Bed'. I've also been wrongly accused of donning royal regalia in Berlin while the Queen was over there on an official state visit, something I would never have dreamt of doing. To this day it amazes me to read that I have appeared on stage in a coffin – as I have made clear, I refused to do so. An American newspaper even concocted a montage of photographs to depict me sitting on the toilet in my regalia. Such efforts abuse the freedom of the press.

Whenever such stories appear, I write to the Queen, enclosing the cutting, and explain that the story is not true. I always receive a letter back from a royal secretary saying that my communication will be placed before the Queen. The Palace are, as we all know, very used to seeing the press make up stories and, to put the record straight, the Palace itself has never complained about my activities.

Many people who employ me to make appearances at events such as anniversaries, birthdays, and barmitzvahs, are themselves wary of upsetting the Palace. Sometimes they ask me if I have ever had any trouble there and I usually suggest they call up to ask. The friendly replies they've received show that the royals harbour no bad feelings towards me and the job I do.

Perhaps because they consider the Queen such a serious person, there are a lot of people in the profession who try to shock me when I am presented in character. They use joke cushions which produce sounds like flatulence, pinch my bottom, or strew toy 'whoopsies' around.

My eldest son, David, used often to find that associates would be more interested in hearing about his mother than in the business in hand. He shrugged that sort of thing off, but got really annoyed when one newspaper asked if they could photograph him in polo gear as Prince Charles.

There was also a time when people would jokingly call Carol, my daughter, Princess Anne. Carol used to want to know about my career only if I was meeting up with pop stars but has now become a great help to me, driving me around the country on many of my engagements and showing a great sense of humour. Whenever she puts a stamp on a letter she says, 'I'm going to lick Mum on the stamps.'

My husband can't understand the lookalike phenomena, and is puzzled by people's fascination with my looks. It has been known to irritate him. Once, when we were on holiday in Weston-super-Mare, we went to a concert and Ken got very annoyed because the audience took no notice of what was going on onstage, just sat staring at me. He started making rude faces at them.

He's very useful when people pretend to be taking pictures of each other when they're really trying to sneak photographs of me. He steps in the way to spoil their view.

When he got tickets for Royal Ascot one year, a band of wild horses would not have dragged me into such a possible confrontation. Ken went on his own, and when he came back said he'd seen the Queen and, for the first time, realised how closely I do resemble her. 'You could be twins,' he said.

We used to love taking boxes at the theatre but it became so uncomfortable to see the audience shuffling around in their seats, whispering, and staring up at us during the interval, that we stopped going. Similar scenes in restaurants have stopped us eating out anything like as much as we used to.

Ken has often been mistaken for the Queen's bodyguard as he was when we turned up without a reservation at the very elegant Verrey's Restaurant in Regent Street. The head waiter asked Ken if we wanted a special table and we were ushered into the far corner of the restaurant, where our table was screened off. Later, Ken got up to go to the lavatory and a man who followed him in asked if it was wise for the Queen's guardian to leave her alone. The head waiter told Ken he was convinced I was the Queen slipping in for a quiet meal with a bodyguard.

When he drove me to a personal appearance at the Café Royal, he put on a chauffeur's hat as a joke and the other drivers waiting there thought he had delivered the Queen. He insisted I was not the Queen, but because he had parked right outside they thought he must be a royal chauffeur, and pestered him for tit-bits of gossip about Buckingham Palace.

My discovery and 'second career' came at the perfect time for me when I was starting to find I had spare time and could have become just another bored housewife. From being someone with nothing much to look forward to but the next chore, I was transported into a neverending adventure. I waited excitedly for the next telephone call, to see where it would send me. It could be Holland, Spain, Germany, Italy, Singapore, Brazil, Mexico, America, Australia, anywhere. My life was transformed completely and I was amazed to find myself jetted around the world. I was being paid for it, my expenses were being met by whoever employed me, and I was having a fabulous time. I'll let you into a secret: I love my job.

But don't get the idea I spend every moment of my life imitating the Queen. At work I am Jeannette Charles, lookalike to the Queen. At home, I'm a wife and mother.

I'm no female Walter Mitty, and I was determined from the start that I would never lose my own identity. When I'm back at home in Danbury, I switch off my professional image like a light. I do the housework, though I have a lady in once a week to help. I do the cooking, and I'm famous in the family for my home-made cakes. I do the household shopping. I do the gardening. I take our dog for a walk. No, it is not a corgi. He's a lovely Rotweiler called Rocky.

I've also lived long enough in the village for my likeness to the Queen to pass almost unnoticed though there is still the odd awkward moment as when a newcomer to the village recently spotted me in the chemist and blurted out, 'There's the Queen!' Perhaps it should not worry me after all these years, but I can still be embarrassed by this sort of thing.

Sometimes, when I'm out walking the dog, people stop me to ask me to talk to their children, which I'm always pleased to do. If any of the staff at my friendly local bakery make a 'royal' joke, or curtsey, I say, 'Do you mind? I'm not working today.' And from the days of the earliest publicity about me, whenever our dustman saw me he would touch his cap and say, 'Good morning, Your Majesty.' Our milkman also used to say that he delivered 'By Appointment'.

Of course, it is very flattering in a way to be the centre of attention. I have been acknowledged as the person who started the lookalike craze, and the agency who now represent me are called Lookalike, a word which I put into current usage. Some years I've travelled as far as the Queen, and appeared on television as frequently.

We shared adjoining television spots last Christmas Day when I appeared with the TV puppet, Roland Rat, in a programme which immediately preceded the Queen's Broadcast to the Commonwealth. I was shown seated at a desk with a pen and notepad. When Roland Rat asked, 'What are you doing here?' I answered crisply, 'Trying to write my speech.'

One thing my rôle as royal lookalike has shown me is just how tough the Queen's job is. I know how many official engagements she carries out in a year, and the workload is staggering. Looking bright and cheerful throughout them all must be difficult at times. The few hours I spend acting her part fill me with admiration for her full-time performance. Being looked at all the time is exhausting, especially when you have to be permanently conscious of your appearance and presentation. That requires stamina as well as grace.

Her sense of humour is, I know, wry and disarming. I remember the story of Her Majesty calling on a lady friend at a hotel near Sandringham. She arrived in a Land-Rover, wearing riding kit and a headscarf. A woman guest said, 'Please excuse me, but you look remarkably like the Queen.' The reply, delivered without a moment's hesitation, was: 'Thank you. That is very reassuring.'

I am an ardent supporter of the royal family, and I know how much they, and the Queen in particular, are loved and respected. Whenever I appear in character, I feel the great tide of warmth and love which upholds Her Majesty. I share that deep affection for a wonderful woman and her family. They are precious to us all, and make a great contribution to our lives.

So, when I think of the Queen, I say in all sincerity: Long may she reign!